ART GLASS NOUVEAU

Lava Tiffany vase signed *L. C. Tiffany, Inc. Favrile, 6492 M, Exhibition Piece,* 4 3/4″, Chrysler Art Museum.

RAY AND LEE GROVER

ART GLASS NOUVEAU

CHARLES E. TUTTLE COMPANY: Publishers
Rutland, Vermont

Representatives
Continental Europe: Boxerbooks, Inc., Zurich
British Isles: Prentice-Hall International, Inc., London
Australasia: Paul Flesch & Co., Pty. Ltd., Melbourne
Canada: M. G. Hurtig Ltd., Edmonton

Published by the Charles E. Tuttle Company, Inc.
of Rutland, Vermont & Tokyo, Japan
with editorial office at
Suido 1-chome, 2-6, Bunkyo-ku, Tokyo, Japan

First edition, 1967

Book plan by Roland A. Mulhauser
Plate layout by S. Katakura

Liberary of Congress Catalog Card No. 67-10197

Printed in Japan

To

SALLY, DONNA, and JOYCE

CONTENTS

INTRODUCTION

The aim of this book is to present in color, identifiable and collectible art glass produced during the latter part of the 19th and first part of the 20th century. We have endeavored to cover the field from three separate approaches: 1) shape, 2) color, and 3) texture or finish.

Most of the glass illustrated was individually hand made, no two shapes or colors being absolutely identical. However a few categories of blown molded glass produced in this same period are included.

In selecting the items to be shown we endeavored to picture the rarities in each class, as it is usually these quality pieces that separate a collection from an accumulation. When we had a choice of a signed or unsigned similar piece, such as in the Webb cameo group, we decided upon the signed glass of unquestioned origin. Workmen employed at more than one factory during their career would naturally produce similar work in more than one glass house.

Signatures are in italics, as they appear on the piece itself. Please note the height only is shown in inches, no diameters or widths being given. Measurements for practicality, are to the nearest one-quarter inch. There may be a small difference between a pictured article and a similar one you may have, because of individual workmanship.

We strongly urge you to visit personally the museums listed as well as other museums having art glass exhibits.

Every piece shown was individually handled and examined, as well as many thousands of others which were made available to us by all our friends, and by collectors who were most gracious, helpful, and cooperative.

ACKNOWLEDGEMENTS

QUITE OBVIOUSLY this book could never have been written without the opportunity afforded us by our many friends among the collectors, dealers, and museum officials who allowed us to examine all their private "untouchables." With the exception of the photographs of their collection furnished by Mr. and Mrs. E. F. Gore, all photography was done by the authors. Many hours were required at each stop along the way, and without exception everyone went out of their way to make available for our personal handling and examination every piece having any interest to us at all. No cabinet or showcase ever remained locked, and again, without fail, we were invited to make ourselves at home with every collection without reservation.

In addition to the collectors and dealers whose pieces we give acknowledgement to under each picture, we wish especially to extend our thanks to the following: Mr. Bob Rockwell and Mr. Harry Hanley of The Rockwell Galley; Mr. James Mowry and Mrs. Robert Mowry of The Milan Historical Museum; Mr. Ronald Kuchta, Curator, and Nancy O. Merrill, Assistant Curator of The Chrysler Museum of Art; Mary Ann Colado of Rollins College; Mr. Paul N. Perrot, Director, and Mr. Kenneth Wilson, Curator of the Corning Museum of Glass, and Mr. James J. Kux.

ART GLASS NOUVEAU

Amberina

Plates pp. 19ff.

Amberina is generally recognized as a clear yellow glass, shading to red at the top. When the position of the colors are opposite it is known as reverse amberina. In addition to the free blown pieces, there are blown mold types in any number of delightful patterns. Without being technical as to the chemical mix in the glass batch, suffice it to say that when first removed from the fire we have an amber-colored glass. Upon refiring certain portions of the glass, the section refired acquires a reddish shade. If in the refiring an excess amount of heat and time is taken we get an overfired piece which frequently has a gorgeous fuchsia or purple shading. This fuchsia amberina is the most sought after and can be quite exciting in a fine piece.

The New England Glass Company, which acquired the patent rights secured by Joseph Locke in 1883, incised the mark of their initials in a rectangle on a very limited number of their pieces. Their successor company, The Libbey Glass Company, which moved to Toledo, Ohio, marked a great number of pieces by acid etching the word "Libbey."

Almost every glass company in the United States and Europe at some time produced amberina. Other than comparing any given piece of amberina with a broken section dug up from the factory dump, or comparing it with a similar shape which is definitely identified as coming from a specific factory, it is unwise to attribute any particular amberina to any given factory. As a matter of fact, amberina is sought after primarily on the basis of color, and then shape, rather than from a collectible factory source.

There are variations in the amber to red coloring. Combinations may run from blue to red, blue to amber, or green to blue to fuchsia. These colors are achieved by changing the chemical mix in the glass batch, and varying the temperatures at which the pieces are fired. Amberina is normally a single-layered glass.

Understanding the relatively simple color control in the production

Amberina (continued)

of amberina glass permits us to realize that by this color control method of reheating the glass, along with the substitution of different metallic color oxides in the original glass batch, we have no limit in ultimate beauty. Opaque glass, translucent glass with a multiple-layered construction, Mother of Pearl type glass embodying air traps in the glossy, as well as acid-finished types, give us a realization of the potentialities inherent in ingenuity. As evidenced in many examples of undetermined origin but of exciting beauty, it is not difficult to understand that aesthetic talent was certainly not lacking in the artist-workman who created in glass his own painting in color.

* * * * *

Plated Amberina

Plates pp. 23 ff.

Plated Amberina, produced under patents acquired by Joseph Locke in 1886, was made only by the New England Glass Company, Cambridge, Massachusetts. Manufactured for a relatively short time, the finest pieces shade from a golden yellow in the base to a deep fuchsia-red at the top. Two characteristics identify Plated Amberina. First, the ware has a creamy opal lining with frequently an almost-imperceptible blue cast to this lining. Secondly, and in fact the most notable feature, is that it must have vertical, protruding ribs on the outer layer. These pattern-molded ribs may be quite thin or very pronounced and extremely dark in color, but the ribs must be there to be accepted as Plated Amberina. Other than the ribs on Plated Amberina, and without noticing the difference of the white lining in Wheeling Peach Blow, and the creamy opal lining in Plated Amberina, it would be difficult to differentiate between the two wares. Wheeling Peach Blow, however, never has vertical ribs, and Plated Amberina is never without this characteristic. Although we have seen several pieces of ribbed amberina, in fine color, but without any lining, these would be classified as unusually rare exceptions. Technically these pieces would not be included in the category of two-layered Plated Amberina ware.

* * * * *

Mother of Pearl

Plates pp. 25 ff.

Mother of Pearl, abbreviated in descriptions as M.O.P., has, with few exceptions, an outer surface that glows with a lustre finish. The glass is composed of two or more layers, with a pattern showing through to the outside of the piece. This pattern, caused by internal air traps, is created by expanding the inside layer of molten glass into molds with varying designs. Another layer of glass, or coating, brings out the design. This, and succeeding layers of the glass, are then acid dipped, and we have Mother of Pearl Satin Ware.

Patterns are unlimited in number, but the ones most frequently found are the Diamond Quilted (Plates 26, 28, 31, 32, 33, and 34), Herringbone (Plates 19, 35, and 36), Moire (Plate 20), Zipper (Plates

Text cont. on p. 36

1. Amberina covered jar, 8 3/4″, collection of Mr. and Mrs. C. W. Bray.

2. Amberina covered jar signed *Libby*, 4 1/2″, collection of Mr. and Mrs. J. Michael Pearson.

Text on pp. 17–18

3. Amberina engraved creamer, 6″, Chrysler Art Museum.

4. Amberina celery vase, 6 1/2″, Chrysler Art Museum.

5. Amberina creamer, 4″, collection of Maude B. Feld.

Text on pp. 17–18

6. Amberina rope handled pitcher, 7 1/2″, collection of Mr. and Mrs. Gerry Philpot.

7. Amberina fluted top vase, 6 3/4″, collection of Mr. and Mrs. J. Michael Pearson.

Text on pp. 17–18

8. Amberina finger bowl, New England Glass Company, 5″, Chrysler Art Museum.

9. Amberina daisy and button pattern plate, 6″, Milan Historical Museum.

10. Amberina vase with stork pattern designed by Joseph Locke, New England Glass Company, 4 3/4″, collection of Sally A. Rose.

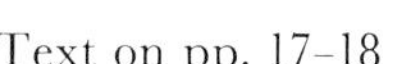

Text on pp. 17–18

11. Plated Amberina pitcher, New England Glass Company, 7″, collection of Mary Mann.

12. Plated Amberina creamer, New England Glass Company, 2 1/2″, collection of Sally A. Rose.

Text on p. 18

13. Plated Amberina syrup, New England Glass Company, 5 3/4″, collection of James N. Donahue.

14. Plated Amberina lemonade, New England Glass Company, 4 3/4″, collection of Mr. and Mrs. C. W. Bray.

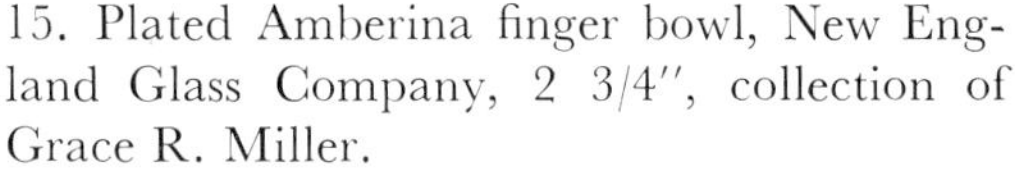

15. Plated Amberina finger bowl, New England Glass Company, 2 3/4″, collection of Grace R. Miller.

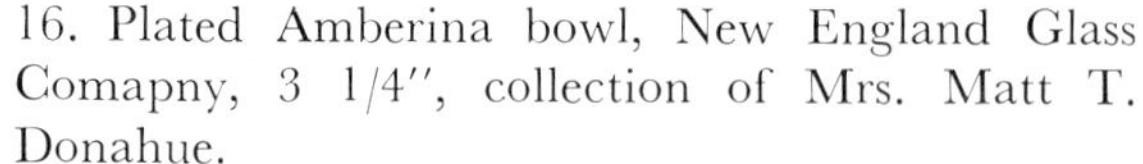

16. Plated Amberina bowl, New England Glass Comapny, 3 1/4″, collection of Mrs. Matt T. Donahue.

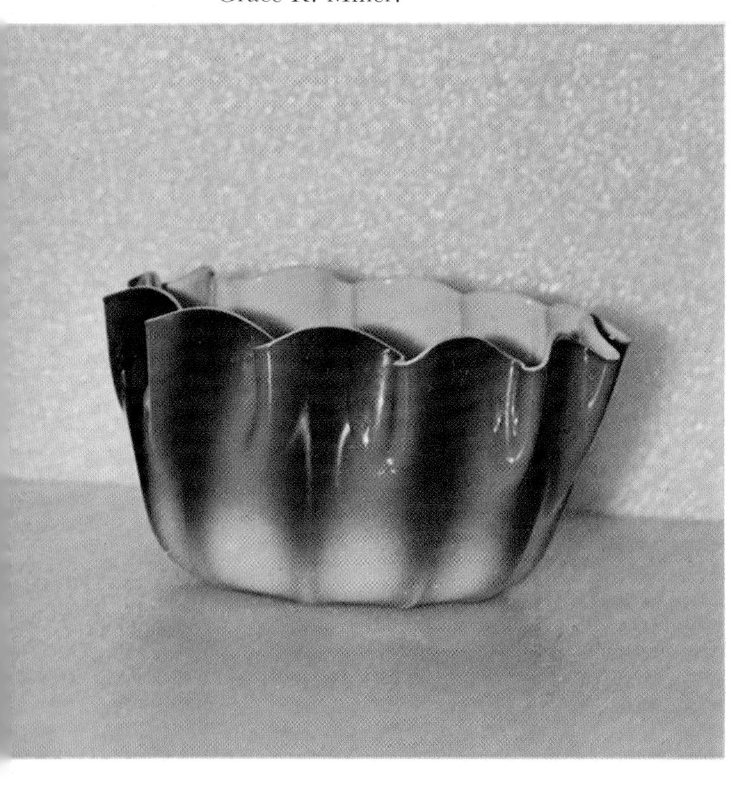

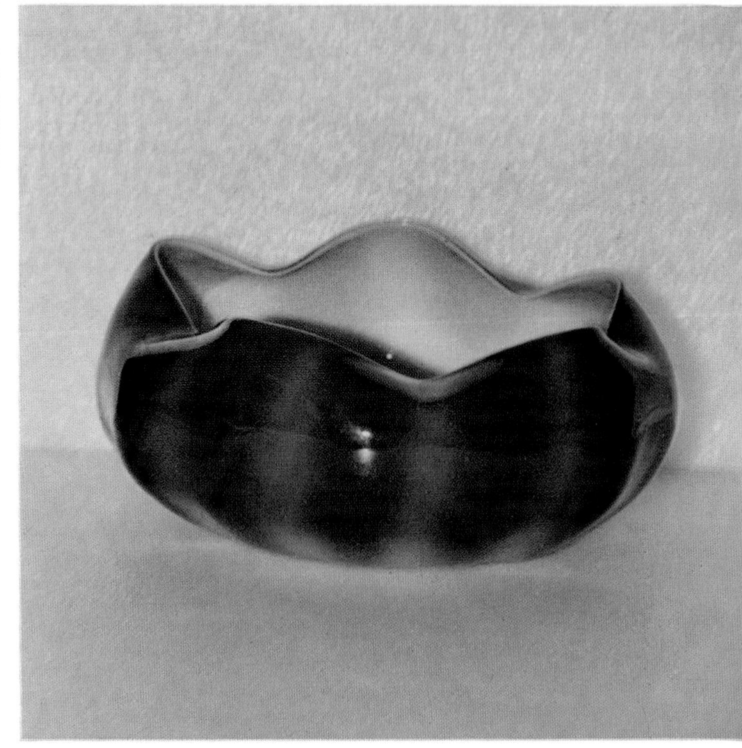

Text on p. 18

17. Mother of Pearl ewer with swirl pattern, 12 1/4″, collection of Sally A. Rose.

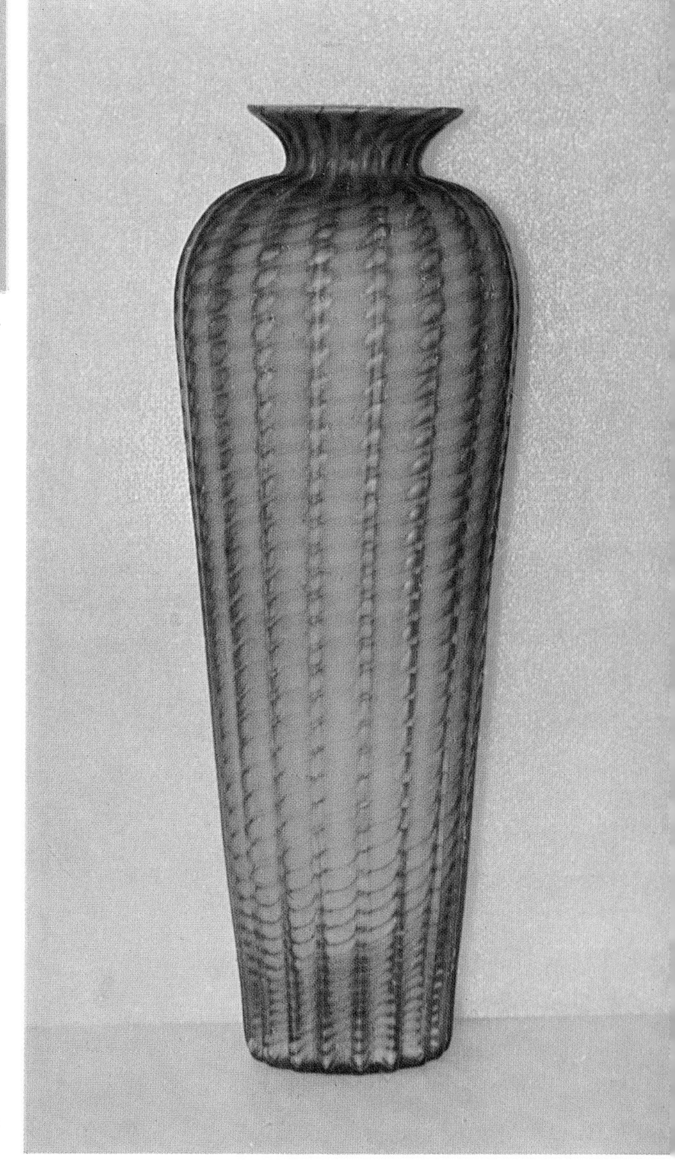

18. Zipper Mother of Pearl vase with chartreuse lining, 16 1/4″, collection of Grace R. Miller.

Text on p. 18

19. Mother of Pearl thorn handled vase with herringbone design, 10″ collection of Sally A. Rose.

20. Mother of Pearl thorn handled basket with moire pattern, 12″, collection of Mr. and Mrs. J. Michael Pearson.

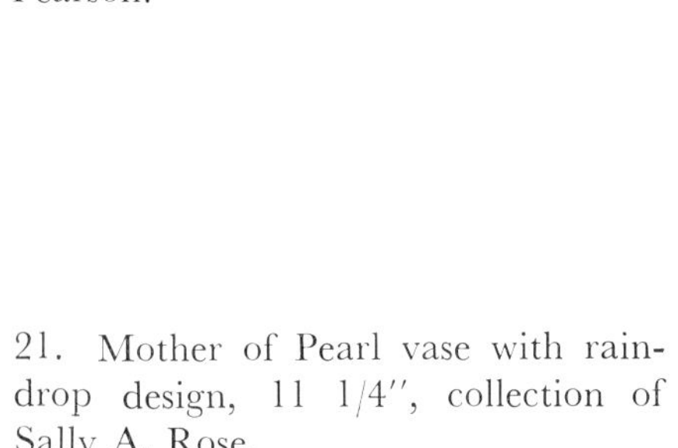

21. Mother of Pearl vase with raindrop design, 11 1/4″, collection of Sally A. Rose.

Text on p. 18

22. Mother of Pearl vase with peacock eye pattern, 8″, collection of Sally A. Rose.

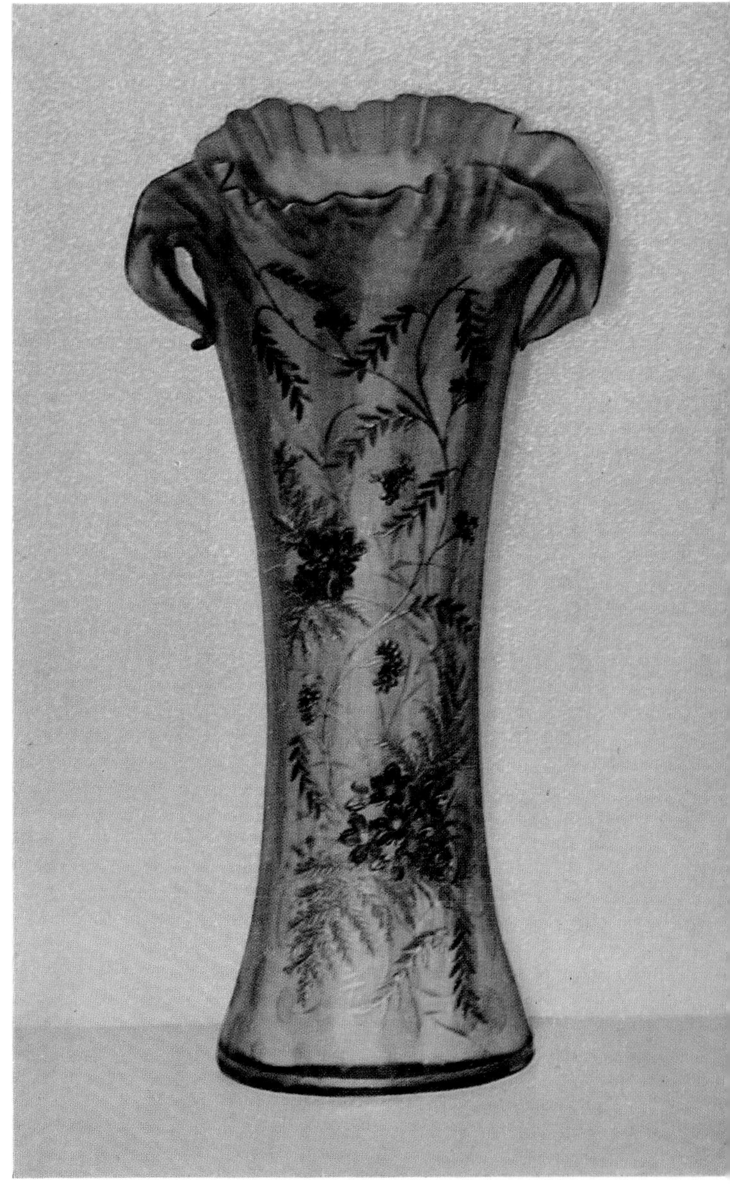

23. Mother of Pearl two-color rainbow decorated vase, 11″, Milan Historical Museum.

Text on p. 18

24. Mother of Pearl vase with flower and acorn design, 10 1/4″, collection of Mr. and Mrs. L. C. Hegarty.

25. Mother of Pearl vase with Federzeichnung design, 6″, collection of Mr. and Mrs. Gerry Philpot.

Text on p. 18

26. Mother of Pearl vase with diamond quilted pattern, 11 3/4″, collection of Sally A. Rose.

27. Mother of Pearl vase with swirl design, 13 1/2″, collection of Sally A. Rose.

Text on p. 18

28. Mother of Pearl stick vase with diamond quilted pattern, attributed to Thomas Webb and Sons, 7 1/4″, collection of Mr. and Mrs. Gerry Philpot.

29. Mother of Pearl hand-shaped vase, 10 1/4″, collection of Maude B. Feld.

30. Mother of Pearl footed vase with zipper pattern, 9 1/4″, collection of Mary Mann.

Text on p. 18

31. Rainbow Mother of Pearl pitcher with diamond quilted design, 7 1/2″, collection of Mr. and Mrs. C. W. Bray.

32. Rainbow Mother of Pearl rosebowl with diamond quilted design, signed *Patent,* 3 1/4″, collection of Mr. and Mrs. C. W. Bray.

33. Rainbow Mother of Pearl lamp with diamond quilted design, 15″, collection of sally A. Rose.

Text on p. 36

34. Rainbow Mother of Pearl footed bowl with diamond quilted design, signed *Patent,* 7″, collection of Sally A. Rose.

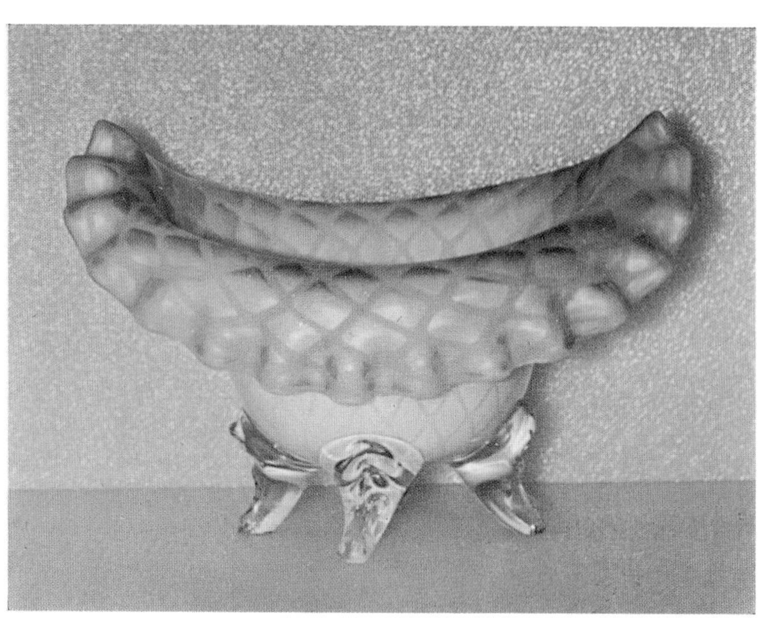

35. Rainbow Mother of Pearl ewer with herringbone design, 8 1/4″, collection of Sally A. Rose.

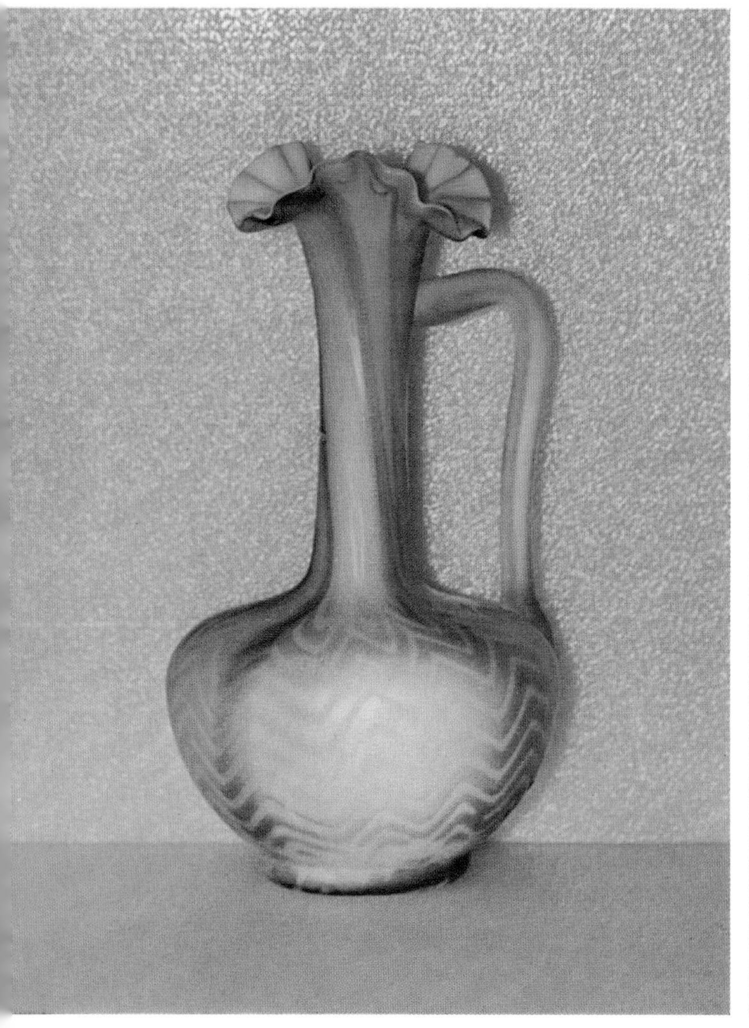

36. Rainbow Mother of Pearl basket with herringbone design, 9 1/2″, collection of Sally A. Rose.

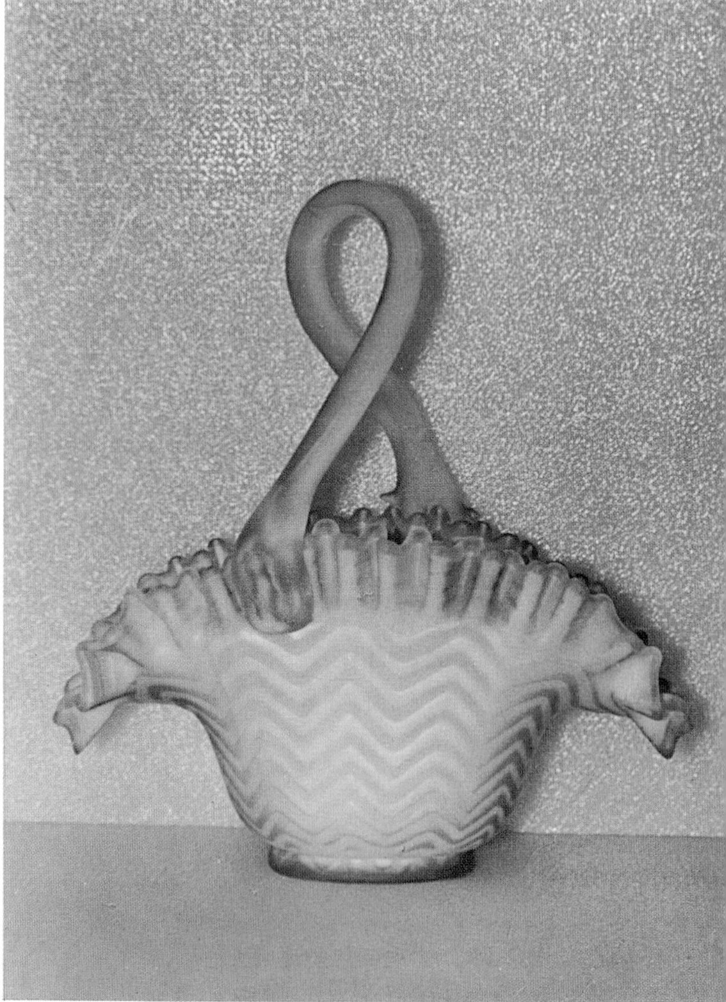

Text on p. 36

37. Burmese glossy cruet and acid finish cruet, Mt. Washington Glass Company, 6 3/4″, collection of Mr. and Mrs. C. W. Bray.

38. Burmese candleholder-vase combination, Mt. Washington Glass Company, 13 1/2″, collection of Grace R. Miller.

39. Burmese handled vase, Mt. Washington Glass Company, 12″, collection of Dr. and Mrs. Walter Donahue.

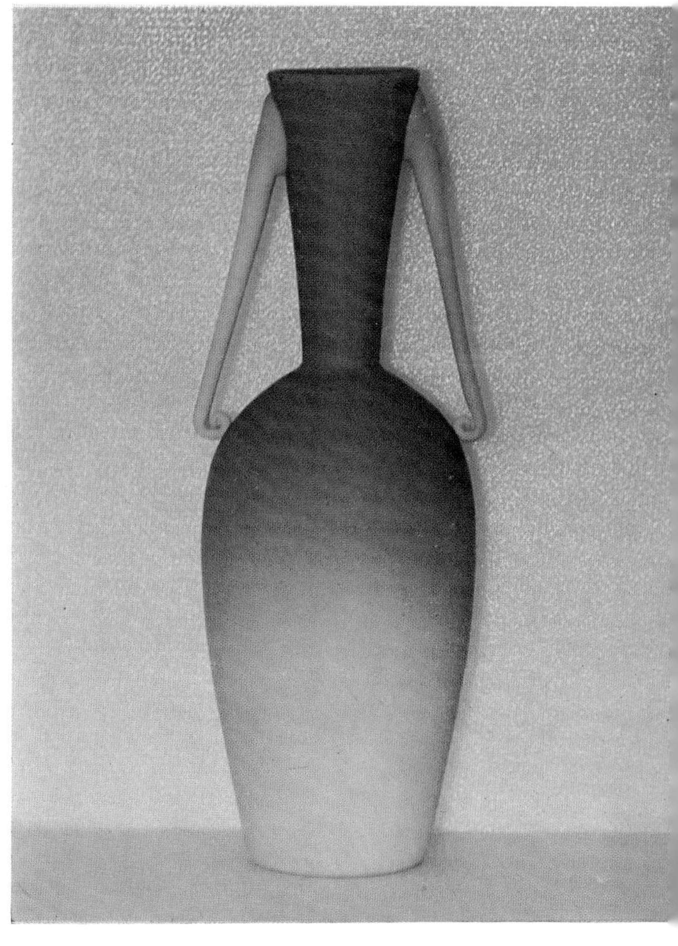

Text on pp. 36–37

40. Burmese vase, Mt. Washington Glass Company, 10″, collection of Mr. and Mrs. E. F. Gore.

41. Burmese lamps and chimney, Mt. Washington Glass Company, 14″, collection of Mr. and Mrs. E. F. Gore.

42. Burmese pieces with "Queen's" design, Mt. Washington Glass Company, 10 1/2″, collection of Mr. and Mrs. E. F. Gore.

Text on pp. 36–37

43. Burmese vase, Mt. Washington Glass Company, 12 1/2″, collection of Mr. and Mrs. C. W. Bray.

Text on pp. 36–37

18 and 30), Swirl (Plates 17 and 27), Raindrop (Plates 21 and 23), Flower and Acorn (Plate 24), Federzeichnung (Plate 25), and Peacock Eye (Plate 22).

Rainbow Mother of Pearl

Plates pp. 31-32

This ware is produced in one solid color, a single color shading light to dark, two colors blended, or a number of colors, including the very handsome rainbow effect. As pictured, Rainbow is found with any number of air trap patterns. All shapes are represented in the Mother of Pearl ware that was produced by most American, English, and European factories. It should also be pointed out that the inner lining is not necessarily white but might be found in color, making for added attractiveness.

In addition, many Mother of Pearl pieces of glass were decorated with colorful enamels, cameos, coralene beading, and other applied glass decorations.

The Mt. Washington Glass Company produced much of this fine ware, and their pieces may be identified by similarity of decoration with that found on Burmese, Crown Milano, and other Mt. Washington glass.

Beauty of color, combined with shape and design, determines quality rather than origin. To some, the firm strong colors are the most desirable, but again the pastels are equally sought after, and thus it becomes completely a matter of personal choice.

* * * * *

Burmese

Plates pp. 33ff.

The Mt. Washington Glass Company, New Bedford, Massachusetts, in 1885 gave the name "Burmese" to a single-layered piece of glass shading from yellow in the base to a salmon pink at the top. When first removed from the fire we have an opaque yellow ware which the workman then proceeds to refire. Sections exposed to this reheating turn pink. A second refiring will cause a return to the original yellow color frequently seen on the rim. Ability of the individual workman to control the shaded coloring determines the quality of the individual piece. With the exception of a few shapes made for daily household use, such as the cruets (Plate 37) which were mold blown, the work was free blown. Some pieces had very finely wrought, applied decorations as shown in Plates 43, 49, and 51, the last one listed showing an exquisite application of "wishbone" feet.

In 1886, one year after patents were first taken out, licenses were issued to Thomas Webb & Sons, England, permitting them to copy as well as to produce their own shapes and designs. While most of the English Burmese was acid finished, Mt. Washington offered this ware in the glossy as well as the acid finish.

There was no limit to pattern decoration, although certain motifs are typical of each factory. Obviously every decorated work was also available in the plain acid and glossy finish, so in endeavoring to cover the field shapewise, we have not hesitated to show many finely decorated pieces.

Steffin, Shirley, Canty, Frederickson, and Knetchel, all associated in various capacities with Mt. Washington, are responsible for many of the original decorative patterns. Guba ducks, so called after the artist of that name, are extremely rare and sought after. Pictured also is the "Queen's design" (Plate 42) made famous by the decoration used on the set of Burmese ordered by Queen Victoria. Verses by many well known poets were also enameled on the ware. Egyptian scenes, bird and animal portrayals, as well as the "fish in the net" decorations are not common. Any decorative work found on other Mt. Washington products such as Crown Milano and Royal Flemish, is quite apt to have been used on Burmese, as the same artists did most of this work.

* * * * *

Crown Milano

Plates pp. 43 ff.

The elegant, painted, and enameled glass named Crown Milano, manufactured by the Mt. Washington Glass Company, New Bedford, Massachusetts, about 1890, was the same ware in texture, shape, and decoration as the earlier glass first called Albertine by the same factory. Other than when identified by perishable paper labels, Albertine cannot be differentiated from unmarked Crown Milano. The initials "C" and "M", one upon the other, usually with a five pointed crown above the initials, and occasionally with numbers underneath, is the Crown Milano trademark.

Made of white opal glass and acid finished, with a varied background of designs in transparent whites, tans, and pastel colorings, Crown Milano was additionally decorated with the familiar floral, figural, animal, bird, and fish motifs of the Mt. Washington Glass Company. These same ornate, decorative themes were used by their artists on all their other types of glass. We strongly urge you to refer to the pictures of Burmese, Peach Blow, Royal Flemish, and Crown Milano, for identification purposes.

One exception to the above description of Crown Milano occurs in the case of the glossy pieces commonly known as Shiny Crown Milano. These, however, may be identified by a fired on red laurel wreath on the underpart of the glass, occasionally with numbers and/or the "C" "M" initials. This ware, a shiny white opal glass, usually has heavy gold colored decoration in a floral motif (Plate 104).

* * * * *

Royal Flemish

Plates pp. 46–47

An unusual glassware named Royal Flemish was manufactured by the Mt. Washington Glass Company, New Bedford, Massachusetts about 1890. The background of this glass is acid finished with heavily

Text cont. on p. 40

44. Burmese hobnail pitcher, Mt. Washington Glass Company, 5 1/2″, collection of Mr. and Mrs. E. F. Gore.

45. Burmese fairy lamp, Thomas Webb and Sons, with two signatures: *Queens Burmese Patented Thomas Webb and Sons,* and *Clarks Fairy, Patent Trademark,* 11 1/4″, collection of Grace R. Miller.

46. Burmese pitcher with verse by Thomas Hood, Mt. Washington Glass Company, 8 3/4″, collection of Mr. and Mrs. C. W. Bray.

Text on pp. 36–37

47. Burmese ewer, Mt. Washington Glass Company, 9 1/4″, collection of Mrs. Matt T. Donahue.

48. Burmese creamer and sugar with wishbone feet, Mt. Washington Glass Company, 3 1/2″, collection of Maude B. Feld.

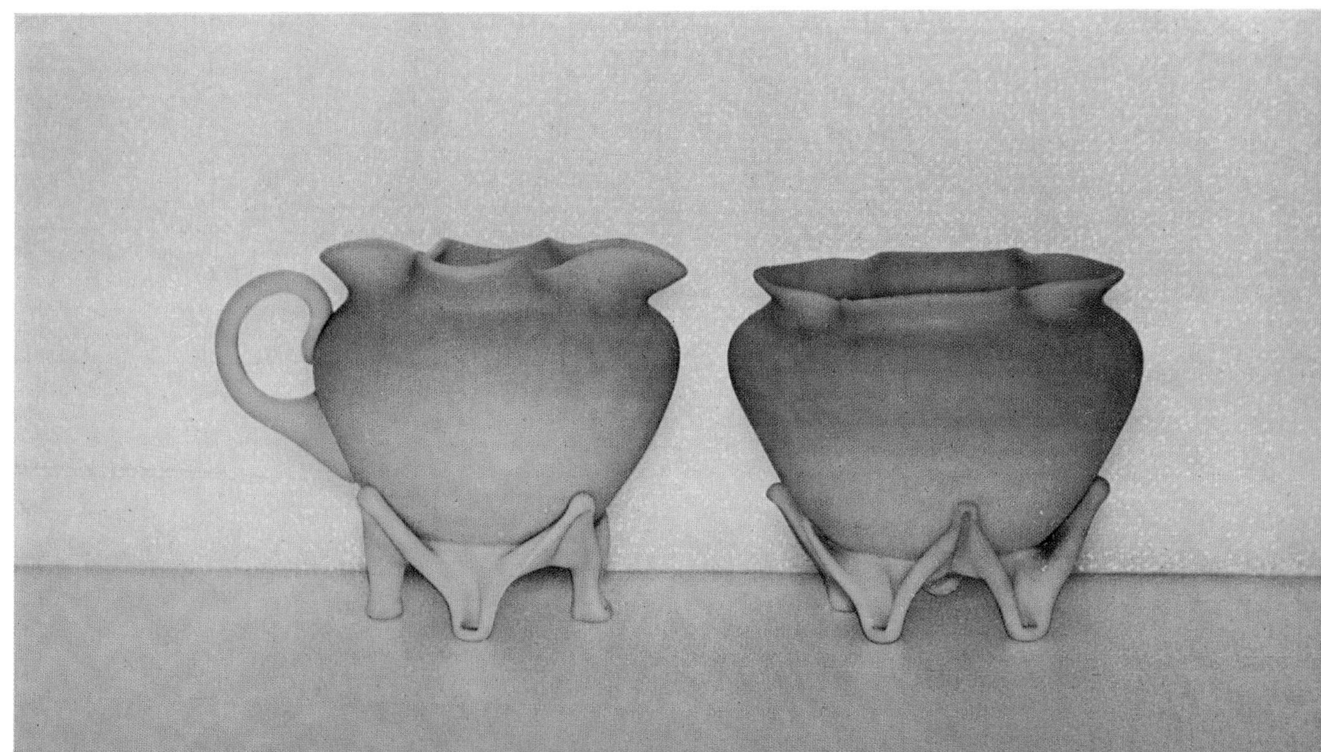

raised gold enameled lines separating each section. It may consist of one or more transparent colors, with the separations giving an overall effect of looking through a stained glass window.

Royal Flemish is noted also for its painted enamels with the designs in high relief, the old Roman motif medallions often being used (Plate 66). Fanciful designs including winged creatures, cherubs, as well as Guba ducks (Plate 62), so-named after the artist who designed them, are highly prized by all collectors.

Shapes and designs follow the standard types in all of the Mt. Washington groups.

When Royal Flemish is marked, the insignia is the "RF," with the initial "R" reversed and backed to the initial "F," enclosed in a four-sided diamond, orange-red in color.

* * * * *

Peach Blow

Plates pp. 48ff.

Chinese porcelain of the late 17th and 18th centuries has been recognized as being superlative in the history of color creation. Subtlety, as well as delicate shading in the finished piece, whether it be in porcelain or glassware, for public display or livability in the home, has not only been accepted but intensely sought after by collectors and the general public alike. Therefore, when in 1886, during an important auction sale of art objects a "Peach Bloom" colored Chinese vase was sold for $18,000.00, the notoriety of the dollar value combined with the seeming magic of the words Peach Bloom triggered manufacturers of colored art glasses to capitalize on the name. Instead of using the name Peach Bloom the spelling was slightly altered to read Peach Blow. There are three main groups, all easily recognized, and several others seldom seen.

New England

Plates p. 48

Type 1, New England Glass Company's Peach Blow, originally known as Wild Rose, is a single-layered glass shading from a red down to a white in the lower part of the piece. The shaded coloring is as noticeable inside the ware as on the outside. Offered in acid, as well as the original glossy finish, the red coloring has a slight purplish cast, particularly on glossy items. The white will frequently shade off to gray.

Mt. Washington

Plates pp. 49–50

Type 2, Mt. Washington Glass Company's Peach Blow, is also a single-layered glass. When the object emerges from the furnace it is of light blue color. Normally the top of the piece is refired and when it is exposed to this refiring heat it becomes pink. We thus have a blue shading to pink ware. When the piece is exposed to acid the surface acquires an all over, slightly gray cast. Being single-layered, the shaded color is the same on the inside as on the exterior of the piece. Most of this ware is found to be acid finished, although quite obviously there must have been some of the pieces that escaped the acid bath in production. Decorated Mt. Washington Peach Blow is extremely rare, and when similar pieces decorated and undecorated were available, we chose the decorated, consistent with our method of selection used throughout the book. As in other fine wares, when a particular and consistent shape or pattern was desired, this was achieved by blowing the molten glass into a mold. Salt and peppers, mustards, and cruets, most of them being ribbed, are obvious examples of this molding process.

Wheeling

Plates pp. 52ff.

Type 3, Wheeling Peach Blow, produced by Hobbs, Brockunier and Co., Wheeling. W. Va., is a two-layered, or lined glassware. The outer layer shades from a golden yellow at the bottom to a mahogany red at the top. This was achieved by refiring the original all-over yellow glass, so that the refired part turned red. The lining consists of a white opal glass, and was in effect the first part of the piece to be formed, with the outer layer shaded from yellow to red glass. The darker red, running somewhat to a fuchsia (purplish), or mahogany color when an excess amount of heat had been applied, is the most desirable color. This is particularly noticeable in acid finished pieces with a narrow neck, where the refiring heat is greatly concentrated during the turning of the piece. The vast majority of pieces found are in the glossy finish, but there still are a fair amount of acid finished examples to be had. In addition to the free form shapes, here again we also have blown molded work. An example of this would be the Wheeling Drape. The piece after being blown into the mold has the Drape pattern, as occurs in a curtain drape. Running from red to white, the ware is identified as Wheeling Drape, but shading from red to yellow, it would be known as Wheeling Peach Blow Drape. While normally a piece would not be really satisfactory without the red to yellow colors having a gradual blend, most pieces of the Peach Blow Drape seem to have a rather marked line, very uneven, practically separating the red to yellow outer shell. Wheeling Peach Blow Drape and Wheeling Drape wares both have the white opal lining found in Wheeling Peach Blow ware. The very expensive Chinese porcelain that sold for $18,000.00 was put up for sale by the executors of the estate of Mrs. Mary Morgan, and the shape of this porcelain vase, when copied by various manufacturers of glass, is known as the Morgan Vase. This Morgan Vase as produced at the New England Glass Company in very limited production, also had the mottled surface decoration known as Agata. Morgan Vases were originally made with amber glass holders. This five-headed griffin molded holder is made of unimportant quality glass and other than being used with and associated with the Morgan Vase could be quite easily overlooked. These stands when perfect are much sought after, but can occasionally be found in homes being used as toothpick holders or just

Text cont. on p. 51

49. Burmese Rigaree decorated bowl, Mt. Washington Glass Company, 4″, collection of Maude B. Feld.

50. Burmese fluted edge bowl, Mt. Washington Glass Company, 4 1/4″, collection of Maude B. Feld.

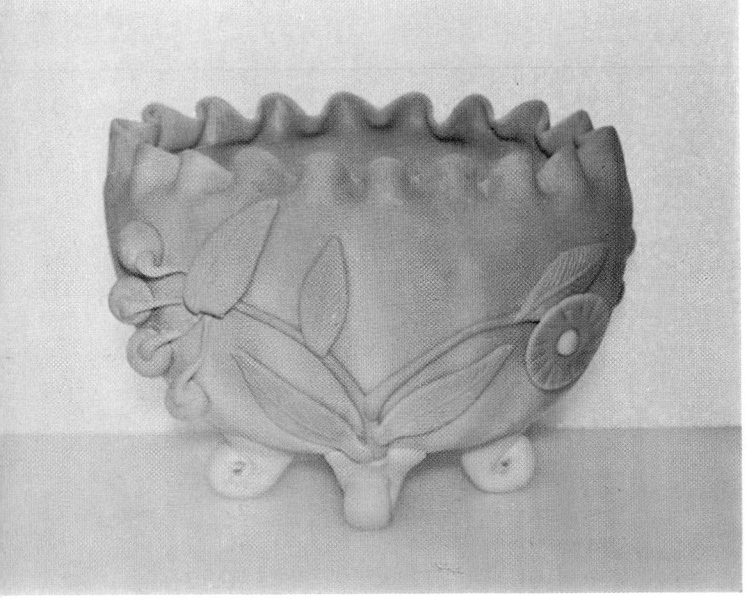

51. Burmese overlay decorated bowl, Mt. Washington Glass Company, 6 1/2″, collection of Grace R. Miller.

52. Burmese syrup, Mt. Washington Glass Company, 6″, collection of Grace R. Miller.

Text on pp. 36–37

53. Crown Milano vase, Mt. Washington Glass Company, signed *C. M.*, 11″, Chrysler Art Museum.

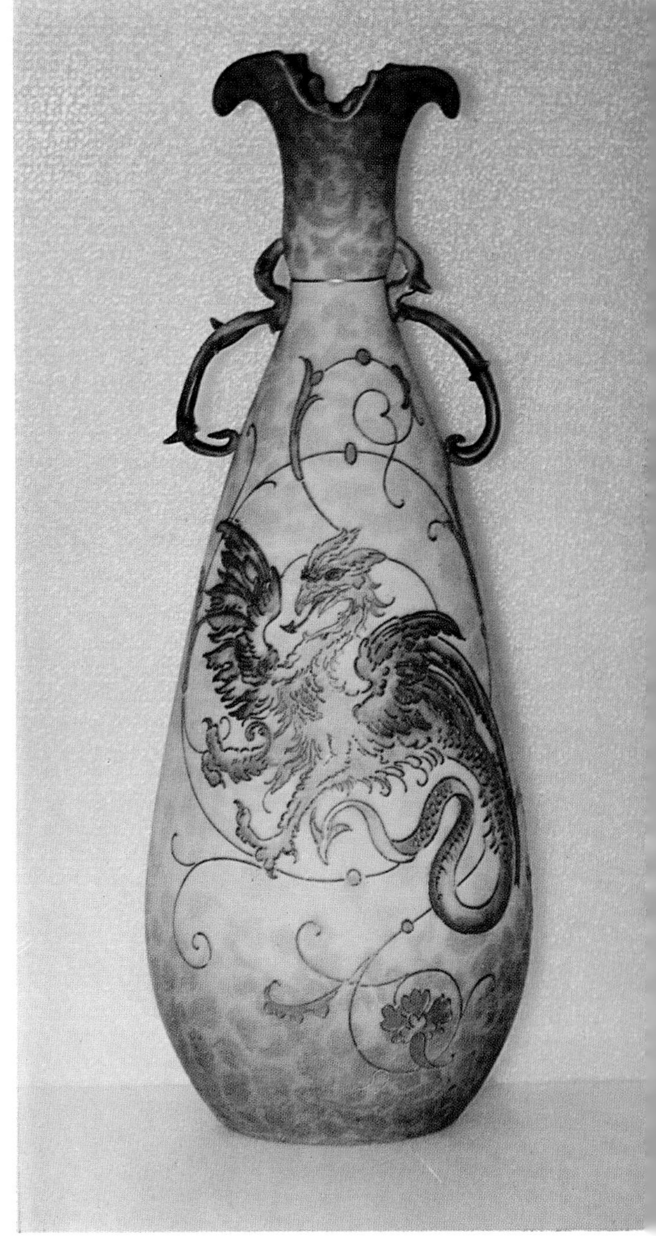

54. Crown Milano vase, Mt. Washington Glass Company, signed 509, 14 3/4″, collection of Dr. and Mrs. Alick Osofsky.

Text on p. 37

55. Crown Milano vase, Mt. Washington Glass Company, signed *580,* 8 1/2″, collection of Dr. and Mrs. Alick Osofsky.

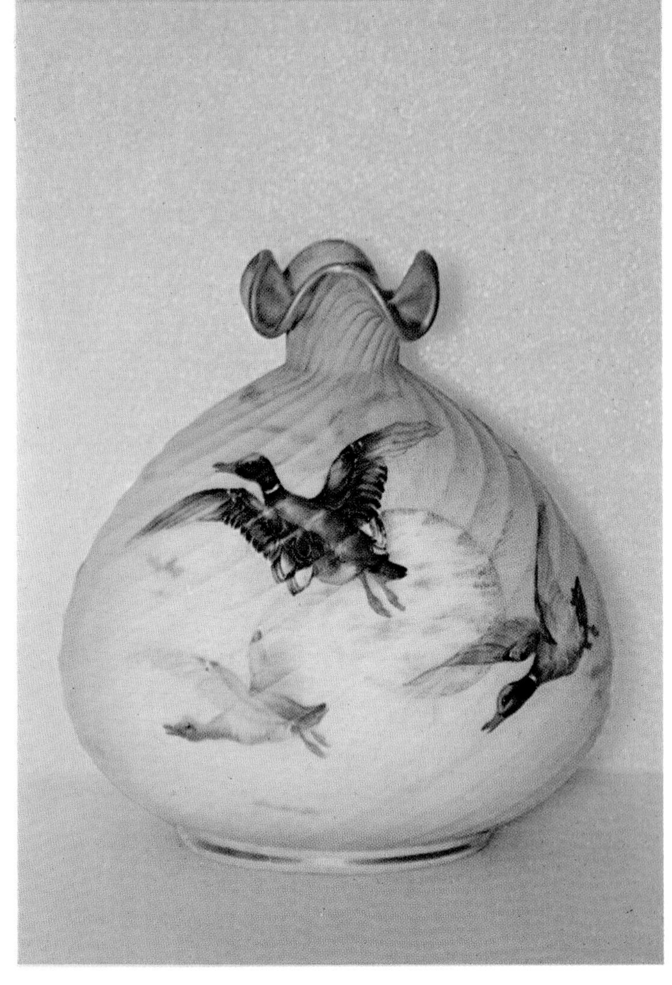

56. Crown Milano rope handled ewer, Mt. Washington Glass Company, signed *C.M. 500,* 10″, collection of Maude B. Feld.

57. Crown Milano pitcher, Mt. Washington Glass Company, signed *C.M. 501,* 12 1/4″, collection of Mr. and Mrs. Gerry Philpot.

Text on p. 37

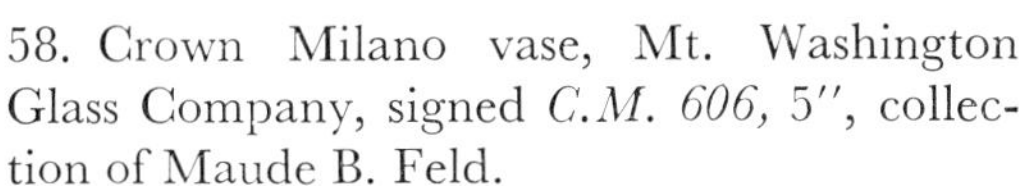

58. Crown Milano vase, Mt. Washington Glass Company, signed *C.M. 606,* 5″, collection of Maude B. Feld.

59 Crown Milano covered vase, Mt. Washington Glass Company, signed *C.M. 530,* 5 1/2″, collection of Mr. and Mrs. Gerry Philpot.

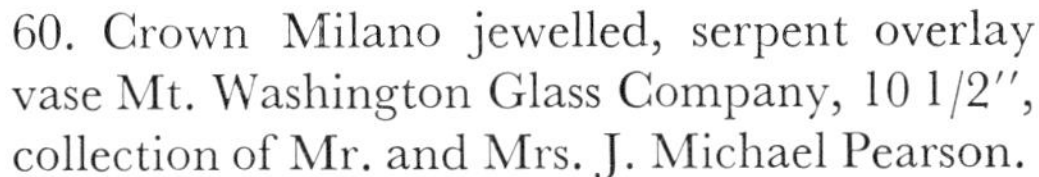

60. Crown Milano jewelled, serpent overlay vase Mt. Washington Glass Company, 10 1/2″, collection of Mr. and Mrs. J. Michael Pearson.

61. Crown Milano covered bowl, Mt. Washington Glass Company, stamped *M.W.* in the metal cover, 8 3/4″, Chrysler Art Museum.

Text on p. 37

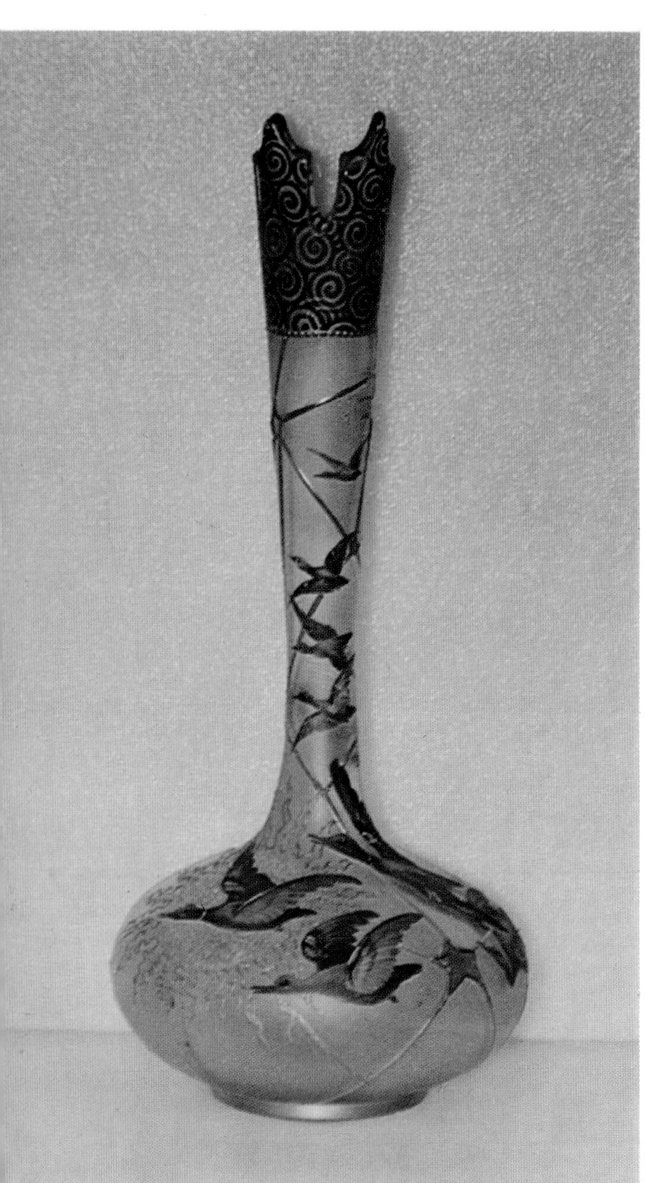

62. Royal Flemish stick vase, Mt. Washington Glass Company, 15″, collection of Mr. and Mrs. Gerry Philpot.

63. Royal Flemish ewer, Mt. Washington Glass Company, 15 1/2″, Milan Historical Museum.

Text on p. 37

64. Royal Flemish pitcher, Mt. Washington Glass Company, 9″, collection of Dr. and Mrs. Walter Donahue.

65. Royal Flemish vase, Mt. Washington Glass Company, 13″, collection of Mr. and Mrs. E. F. Gore.

66. Royal Flemish covered cookie jar, Mt. Washington Glass Company, 9 3/4″, collection of Mr. and Mrs. Gerry Philpot.

Text on p. 37

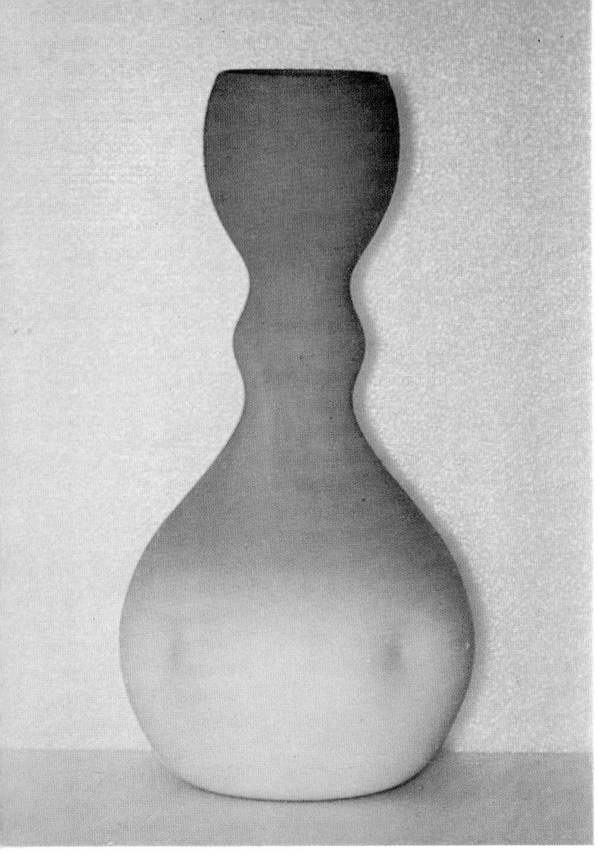

67 (left) Peach Blow acid vase, New England Glass Company, 11″, collection of Sally A. Rose.

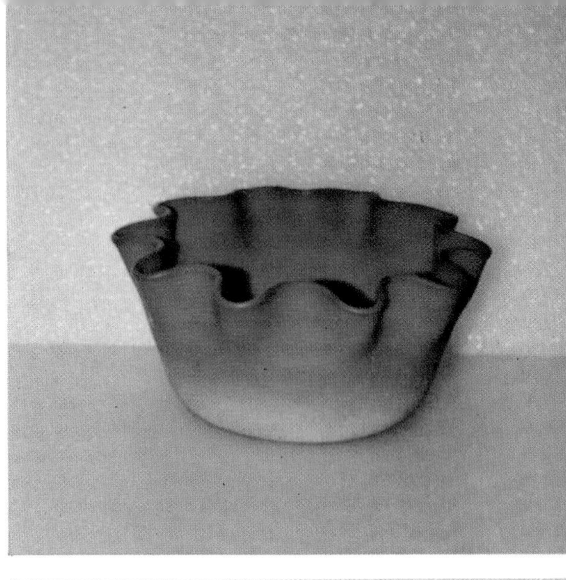

68. (right). Peach Blow acid finger bowl, New England Glass Company, 2 1/4″, collection of Mr. and Mrs. Raymond Suppes.

69 (right). Peach Blow glossy pitcher, New England Glass Company, 6 1/2″, collection of Maude B. Feld.

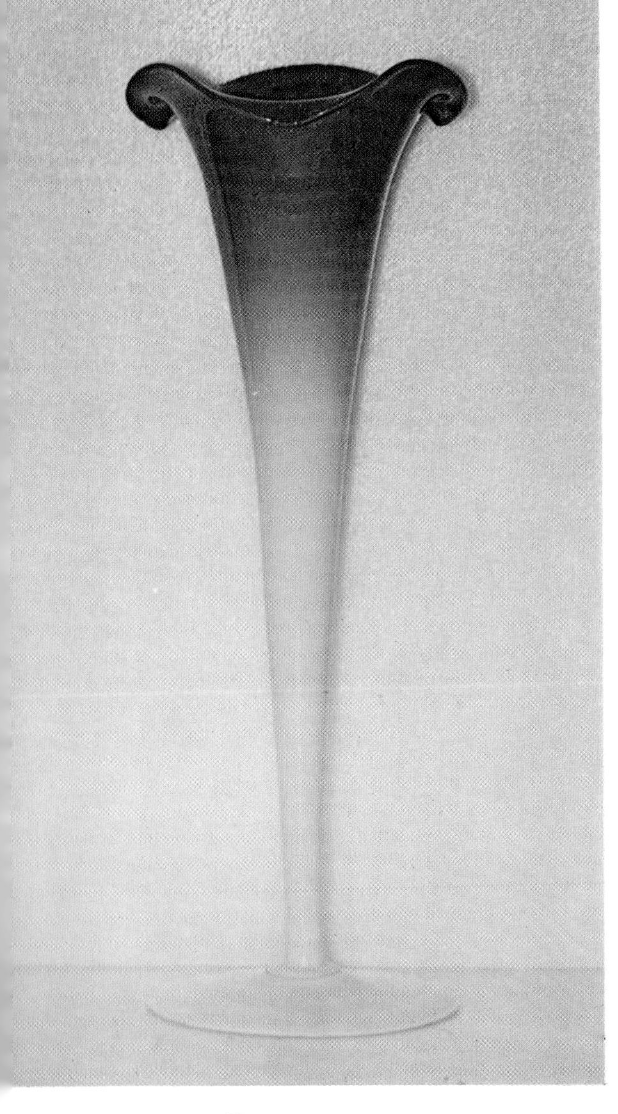

70 (left). Peach Blow glossy lily vase, New England Glass Company, 18″, Chrysler Art Museum.

71 (right). Peach Blow glossy finish and acid finish stick vases, New England Glass Company, 8 1/4″, Chrysler Art Museum.

Text on p. 40

72. Peach Blow pitcher decorated with verse by James Montgomery, Mt. Washington Glass Company, 6 3/4″, collection of Mrs. Matt T. Donahue.

Text on p. 40

73. Peach Blow acid finish, decorated bowl, Mt. Washington Glass Company, 2 1/4″, Corning Museum of Glass.

74. Peach Blow acid finish, crimpled top sugar and creamer, Mt. Washington Glass Company, 5 1/2″, collection of Sally A. Rose.

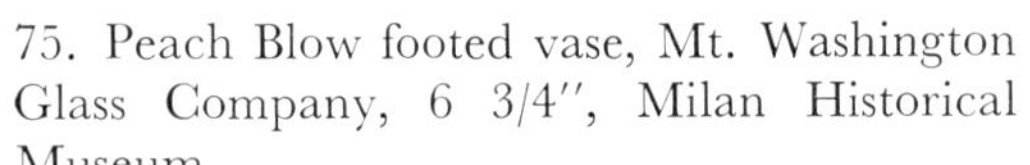

75. Peach Blow footed vase, Mt. Washington Glass Company, 6 3/4″, Milan Historical Museum.

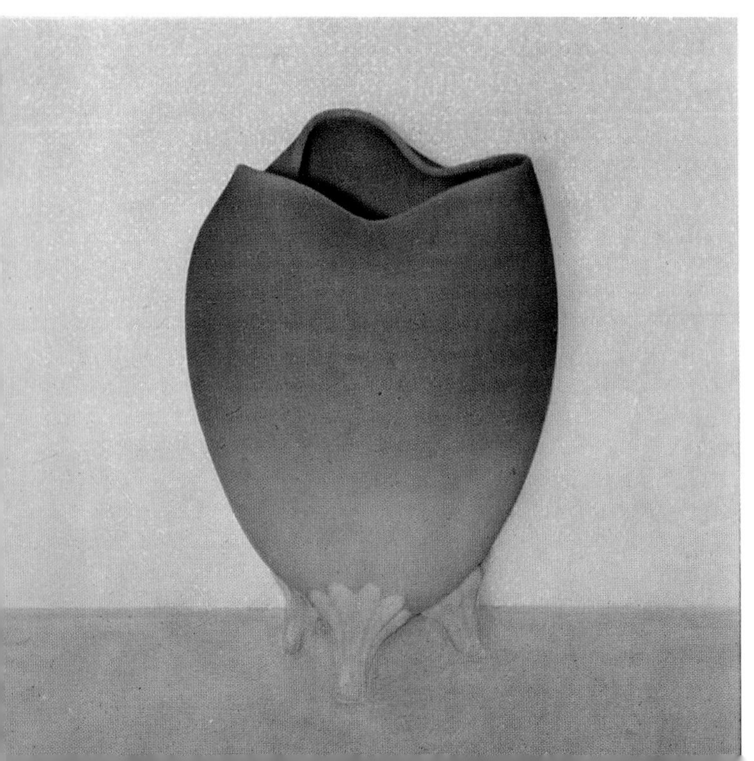

76. Peach Blow acid finish, decorated stick vase, Mt. Washington Glass Company, 7 3/4″, collection of Maude B. Feld.

77. Peach Blow acid finish, decorated lily vase, Mt. Washington Glass Company, 10 1/2″, collection of Mr. and Mrs. E. F. Gore.

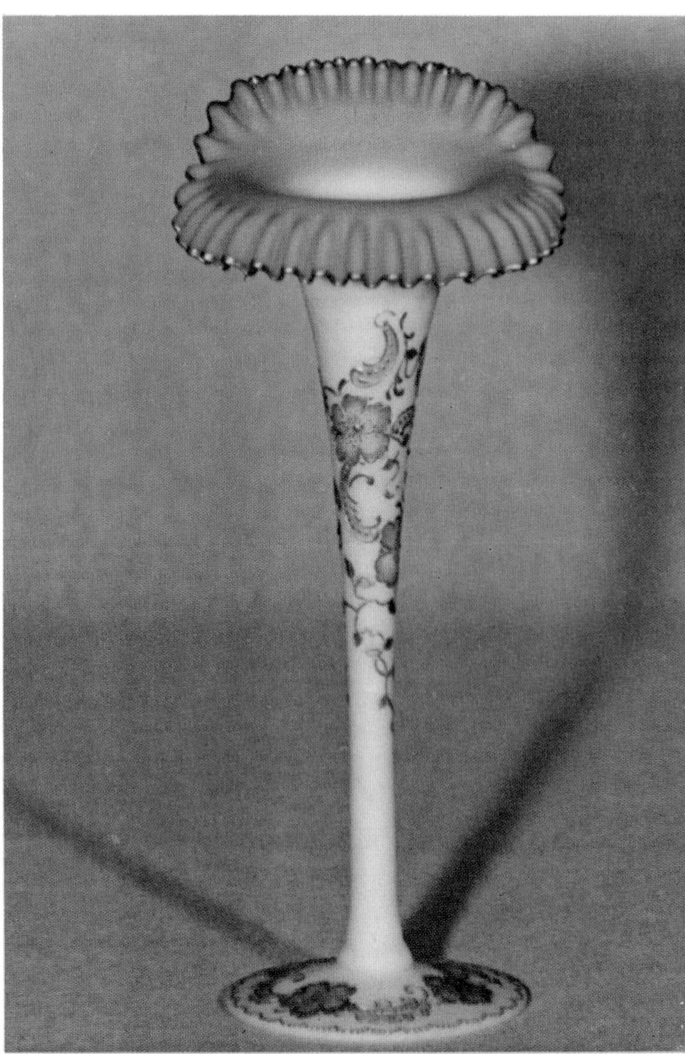

plain ashtrays. They come acid and glossy finished, and are accordingly illustrated.

Type 4, not too common, is the Thomas Webb & Sons, England, Peach Blow (Plate 88). While there is a question as to what color combination is indicated in Webb Peach Blow, that generally accepted consists of a two-layered ware, the outer shell shading from a pink at the base to a deep rich red at the top. The inner lining is an off color cream, having a slightly greenish cast. This was produced in acid as well as a glossy finish, and is frequently found with elaborate gold decoration on both finishes. Occasionally Webb Peach Blow will have the Webb incised mark on the underside. Stevens & Williams, of Stourbridge, England, also produced a Peach Blow similar to Webb, with an occasional mark underfoot.

Thomas Webb

Plate p. 60

Type 5, Sandwich Peach Blow (Plate 89), manufactured by the Boston & Sandwich Glass Company, Sandwich, Massachusetts, on Cape Cod, is a single-layered piece of glass, strawberry ice cream pink in shading, frequently found in a swirl pattern. Internally the color is the same as the outer surface. Overlay decorations are quite usual in a camphor color, with the complete piece having an acid finish.

Sandwich

Plate p. 60

Many other types of glass are loosely termed Peach Blow but the above basic colors do not change, other than a variance of color shading, nor are there differences from the lined and unlined, or single-layered pieces, as "matched up" with the above colors. Unfortunately for would-be hopefuls we must accept that which is generally recognized by collectors and museum curators. In other words, Webb and Wheeling Peach Blow are always lined, but Mt. Washington, New England, and Sandwich Peach Blow are never lined. It is easily understood that for financially practical purposes most glass houses, American as well as foreign, would produce some type of ware termed Peach Blow, and such was the case.

Under patents issued to Joseph Locke shortly after 1885 the New England Glass Company, Cambridge, Massachusetts, produced Agata glass. A metallic stain applied and fired on New England Peach Blow in an allover pattern suggestive of a fanciful golden spiderweb is found on this beautiful Agata ware. With rare exceptions it is only seen on glossy pieces. In addition to the spiderweb mottling some of the pieces also have blackish-blue, so-called "oil spots." These are in demand according to the individual collector's preference.

Agata

Plates pp. 61 ff.

In Plate 92 we show a pair of New England Peach Blow celery vases, one of them with mottling, which we know under the trade name Agata.

To be very specific, Agata, made exclusively by the New England Glass Company, has a mottled design that was applied to plain New

Text cont. on p. 54

78. Wheeling Peach Blow drape pattern pitcher, Hobbs, Brocunier and Company, 5 1/4″, collection of Mr. and Mrs. C. W. Bray.

79. Wheeling Peach Blow acid pitcher, Hobbs, Brocunier and Company, 7″, collection of Mr. and Mrs. C. W. Bray.

Text on p. 41

80. Wheeling Peach Blow glossy sugar and creamer, Hobbs, Brocunier and Company, 10″, collection of Mr. and Mrs. C. W. Bray.

Text on p. 41

England Peach Blow, and is found in any New England Peach Blow shape. Richness of color and fine condition of the mottling determines the overall quality of each piece.

* * * * *

Green Opaque

Plates p. 64

Green Opaque glass, a product of the New England Glass Company, Cambridge, Massachusetts, appeared on the market about 1887. Being a single-layered piece of glass, obviously opaque as the name indicates, the color has the same intensity on the inside of the ware as on the outside. Prior to the final heat a blue mottled stain was applied to the upper part of the various pieces, subsequently to be decorated with a narrow gold border along the lower part of the mottling. Continuous handling will cause this blue mottling to wear thin as the stain had only a slight penetration. In addition to the shapes made for everyday use we do occasionally find simple vase forms. Green opaque is an acid finished ware but like all glass having this finish, glossy examples might be found. Color intensity varies and it should be noted that stoppers for cruets are rarely the same color as the containers themselves, being usually of a much deeper shade of soft green.

* * * * *

Pomona

Plates pp. 65-66

Under patents received by Joseph Locke, in 1885, the New England Glass Company, Cambridge, Massachusetts, produced a ware of extreme delicacy. There has been some confusion about Pomona glass because of two different methods of production.

Found in practically every shape, the original clear glass was subjected to a yellowish metallic stain fired around the upper border of the pieces. On the main body of the glass were small floral designs, of transparent colored metallic stains, frequently blue, as in the cornflower pattern, but also in conjunction with delicate enamel decorations as found in the blueberry pattern. The balance of the glass consists of an all over etching.

To clear up the confusing terminology of "first grind" Pomona as against "second grind" we should understand the difference in manufacturing.

"First grind" etching was accomplished by covering the glass with an acid resistant coating into which was carved thousands of minutely engraved lines. The piece was then dipped into acid that cut into the glass where the workman had carved these lines. This is known as "first grind" and has considerable brilliance. Individual engraved lines may easily be seen with a low power magnifying glass.

Due to the expense of this operation a quicker and cheaper method of acid etching was achieved by rolling the piece in very fine particles of acid resistant material that adhered to the glass. When the piece was then dipped into acid and where there was no protection by the acid resistant particles, a speckled acid etching resulted. This was "second grind" Pomona, which is somewhat less brilliant in appearance.

The cornflower design was used in both "first" and "second" grind, but many other decorations were only produced in the less expensive "second grind" process.

Repeated washing with scouring powder will wear off the transparent colored metallic stain. "First" or "second" grind acid etching will not be affected by wear. Quality is governed by the present condition of the original coloring. Not all Pomona was decorated, many pieces being just acid etched. This glass has a subtle beauty and fascination which attracts many collectors.

* * * * *

Mt. Washington

Plates pp. 67–68

In addition to the better known productions of the Mt. Washington Glass Company, New Bedford, Massachusetts, which include Burmese, Peach Blow, Crown Milano, and Royal Flemish covered elsewhere in this book, they offered a number of other interesting wares in the art glass field to the public.

Noticeable in the pictures, these wares showed a similarity of decoration to that found on the fine work previously described. Plate 108 illustrates what could best be termed Mt. Washington decorated clear glass. These clear pieces have decorations almost identical to those found on some of the Mt. Washington Burmese ware.

White satin glass with fine enamel decoration was another item. We show a shaded piece (Plate 109) with the typical "fish in net" design very effectively portrayed.

Most of the undecorated white satin glass had little decorative appeal. Lack of color might account for its reluctant acceptance by the public.

Napoli glass, so signed underfoot (Plate 107), is a clear glass decorated inside and out. In the piece pictured there is a chrysanthemum floral decor, while the outer side of the piece has a gold lineal pattern reminiscent of that found on Royal Flemish. This one characteristic of a double decoration, inside and out, on the same piece of glass would identify this type of work as being Napoli.

Verona glass (Plate 105) is also a clear glass with a thin, almost washlike painting. Actually it would seem that the pattern desired was covered by wax and the balance of the piece was exposed to an all over spray. When this process was completed the wax was removed and the resulting clear glass became the actual pattern decoration. The smoky tan color on the ware is also quite similar to the color of the larger flat color masses used in Royal Flemish work.

Lava glass, also known as Sicilian ware (Plate 103), is shown in the

Text cont. on p. 58

81. Wheeling Peach Blow acid decanter, Hobbs, Brocunier and Company, 9″, collection of Mr. and Mrs. C. W. Bray.

82. Wheeling Peach Blow glossy pitcher, Hobbs, Brocunier and Company, 10″, collection of Mr. and Mrs. C. W. Bray.

Text on p. 41

83. Wheeling Peach Blow glossy finish and acid finish "Morgan" vases in stands, Hobbs, Brocunier and Company, 10", collection of Mr. and Mrs. C. W. Bray.

Text on p. 41

Mt. Washington (continued)

acid finish. It was also produced with a glossy surface, never having been exposed to an acid bath. Lava glass, basically, is pitch black. The colors shown in the picture are not enamels, but rather colored pieces of random shaped glass, inlaid in a very narrow, thin, white backing.

Regarding Shiny Crown Milano (Plate 104), Please refer to the description of Crown Milano.

The Mt. Washington Glass Company also produced a red and white as well as a blue and white cameo glass. Two of the relatively few patterns used (Plates 102 and 106) are shown. These patterns were duplicated in both color combinations. Cameo work produced by Mt. Washington cannot be confused with the English cameo work because, outside of the carefully cut outline of the cameo decoration, there is a minimum of additional carving or shading by cutting tools so typical of the fine English cameo work.

* * * * *

C.F. Monroe

Plates pp. 69–70

The C. F. Monroe Company, Meriden, Connecticut, in 1898 started to offer the public their Wave Crest Ware, Nakara, and Kelva, all marked pieces. It would be difficult to differentiate between the three types, other than their markings.

Basic opal white glass purchased from outside glass manufacturers was decorated and marketed by the C. F. Monroe Co. Wave Crest is seen in both glossy and satin finishes (Plates 110 and 112), These three types of ware would seem to call for a combination art and commercial classification. Certainly the decorations were not of a commercial nature, but very similar to the earlier Mt. Washington Glass Company's fine artistic work. Shapewise, however, the products were made for primarily utilitarian purposes such as containers for jewels, hair ornaments, collars and cuffs (Plate 113). There is nothing amateurish in the colorful patterns and scenes, but on the contrary they suggest an overall operation by a very demanding and exacting management.

* * * * *

Smith Brothers

Plates p. 71

Brothers Alfred E. and Harry A. Smith operated the decorating department for the Mt. Washington Glass Company, New Bedford, Massachusetts, in 1871. Three years later they acquired control of this decorating department, and in 1878 severed connections and became neighbors of the Mt. Washington Glass Company, operating as the Smith Brothers.

Opal glass blanks were purchased from various sources including the Mt. Washington Glass Company. Much of the work decorated in the Smith Brothers plant can only be identified by comparison with known and signed pieces. The Smith Brothers signature consisted of a stamped "rampant lion in a shield" and the words "trade mark." In addition to their beautiful vases and bowls, the Smith Brothers worked

Text cont. on p. 75

84. Wheeling Peach Blow glossy syrup, Hobbs, Brocunier and Company, 7″, collection of Mr. and Mrs. C. W. Bray.

85. Wheeling Peach Blow acid teardrop cruet, Hobbs, Brocunier and Company, 7″, collection of Mr. and Mrs. C. W. Bray.

86. Wheeling Peach Blow acid tumbler, Hobbs, Brocunier and Company, 3 3/4″, collection of Mr. and Mrs. C. W. Bray.

87. Wheeling Peach Blow acid stick vase, Hobbs, Brocunier and Company, 8 1/4″, collection of Mr. and Mrs. C. W. Bray.

Text on p. 41

88. Peach Blow glossy finish punch bowl, Thomas Webb & Sons, 10 1/2″, cóllection of Mr. and Mrs. Gerry Philpot.

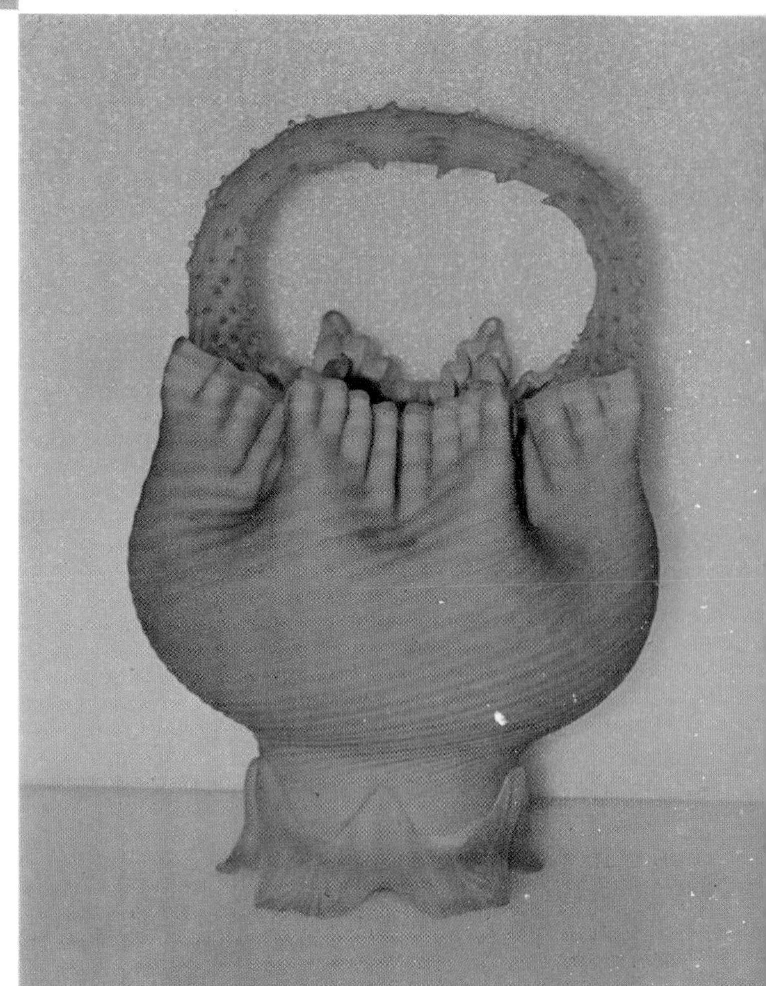

89. Sandwich Peach Blow thorn handled basket with camphor overlay on foot and rim, 10 1/2″, Chrysler Art Museum.

Text on p. 51

90. Agata pitcher, New England Glass Company, 7 1/2″, collection of Mr. and Mrs. C. W. Bray.

Text on p. 51

91. Agata cruet, New England Glass Company, 6″, collection of Maude B. Feld.

92 (lower right). Agata and Peachblow celeries, before and after the Agata decoration, New England Glass Company, 6 3/4″, collection of Maude B. Feld.

93 (left). Agata "Morgan" vase in acid holder, New England Glass Company, 10″, collection of Sally A. Rose.

Text on p. 51

94. Agata lily vase, New England Glass Company, 8″, collection of Sally A. Rose.

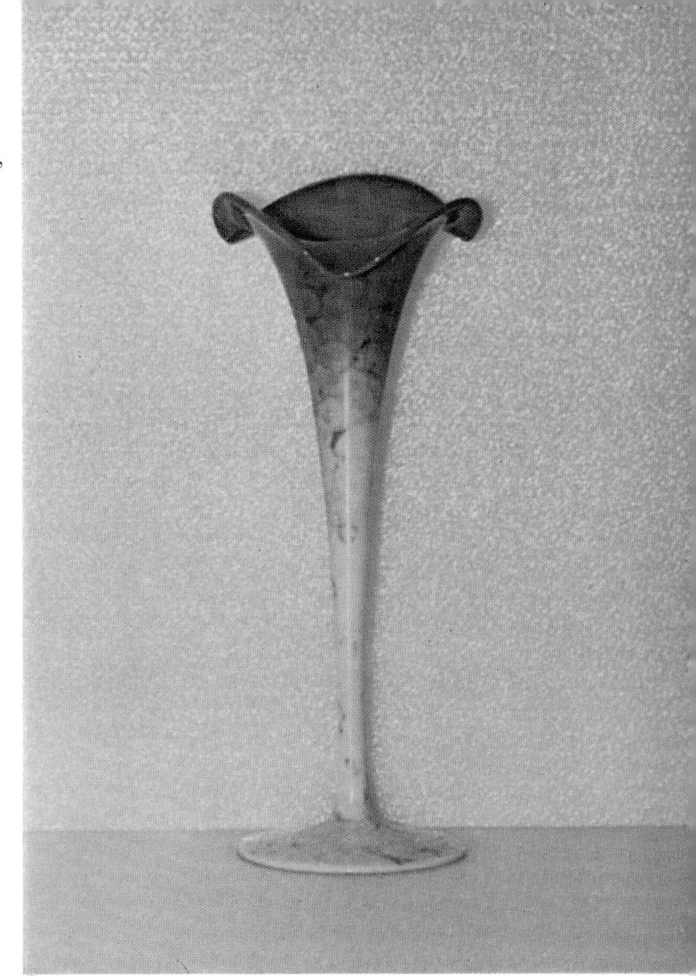

95. Agata stick vase, New England Glass Company, 8 1/4″ collection of Mr. and Mrs. Raymond Suppes.

Text on p. 51

96. Green Opaque bowl, New England Glass Company, 2 3/4″, collection of Mrs. Matt T. Donahue.

97. Green Opaque creamer, New England Glass Company, 3 3/4″, collection of Maude B. Feld.

98. Green Opaque cruet, New England Glass Company, 4 3/4″, collection of Mr. and Mrs. C. W. Bray.

Text on p. 54

99. First grind Pomona butterfly and wheat decoration pitcher, New England Glass Company, 12″, collection of Dr. and Mrs. Walter Donahue.

Text on pp. 54–55

100. Second grind Pomona cornflower decoration goblet, New England Glass Company, 5 3/4″, collection of Maude B. Feld.

101. Second grind Pomona blueberry decoration spooner, New England Glass Company, 4 3/4″, Chrysler Art Museum.

Text on pp. 54–55

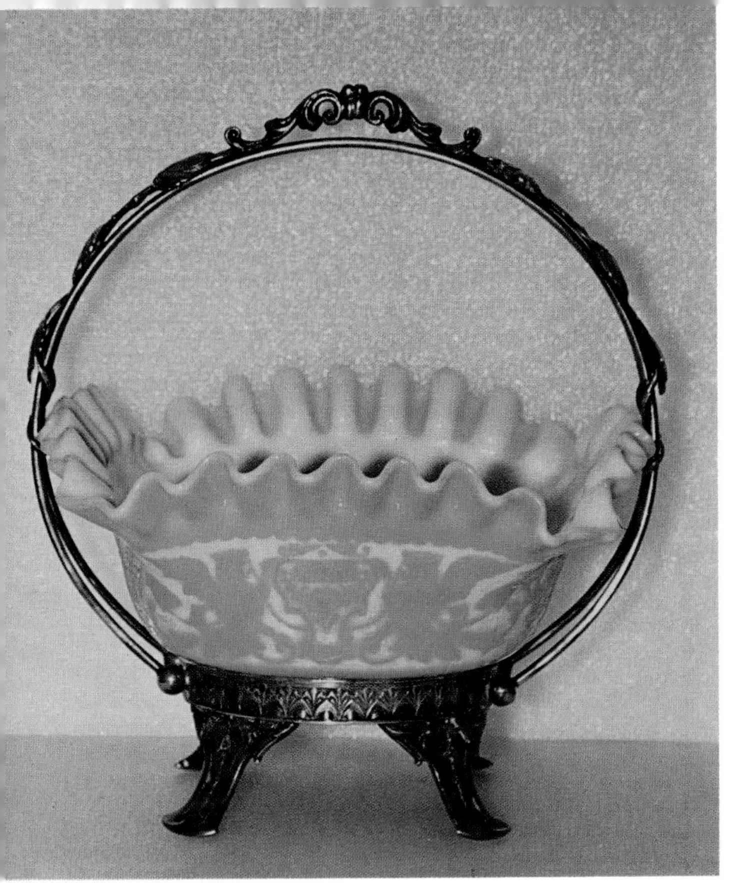

102. Cameo brides basket, Mt. Washington Glass Company, 10″, collection of Dr. and Mrs. Alick Osofsky.

103. Lava glass, satin finish vase, Mt. Washington Glass Company, 8 3/4″, Milan Historical Museum.

104. Shiny Crown Milano pitcher, Mt. Washington Glass Company, signed in red enamel decoration of *wreath and number 1025,* 9 1/2″, collection of Mr. and Mrs. Gerry Philpot.

105. Verona glass fluted vase, Mt. Washington Glass Company, signed *Verona,* 14″, authors' collection.

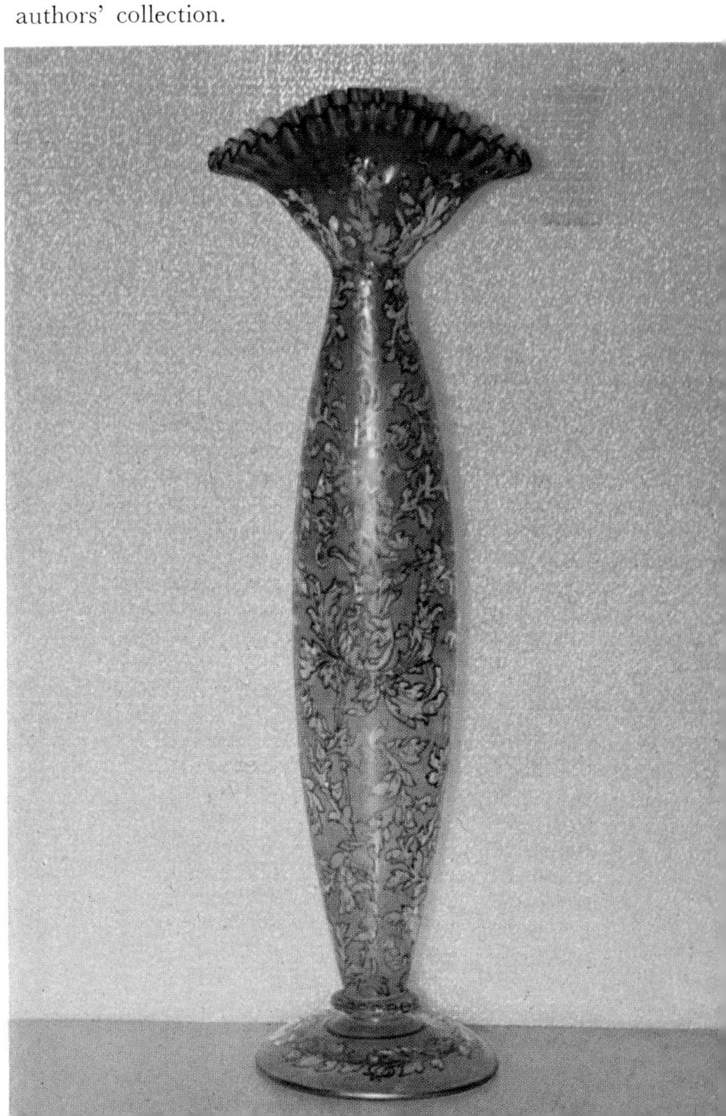

106. Cameo vase, Mt. Washington Glass Company, 4 3/4″, collection of Mr. and Mrs. Gerry Philpot.

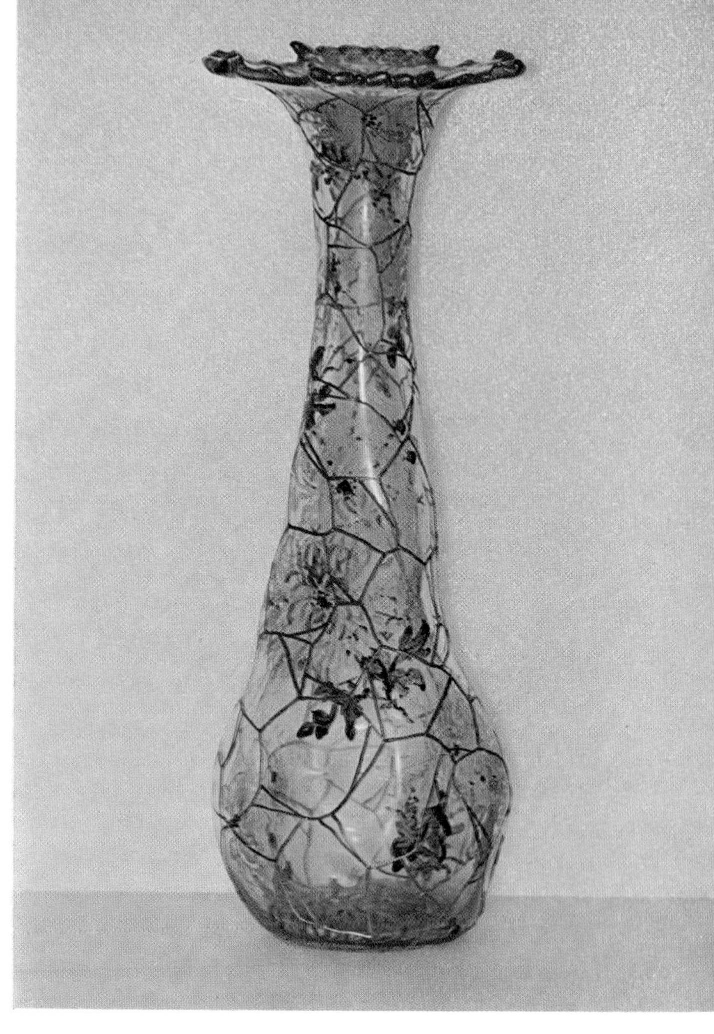

107. Vase, Mt. Washington Glass Company, signed *Napoli* 829, 15 1/2″, Chrysler Art Museum.

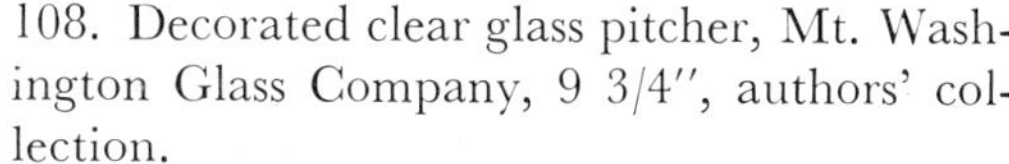

108. Decorated clear glass pitcher, Mt. Washington Glass Company, 9 3/4″, authors' collection.

109. White satin glass vase, Mt.Washington Glass Company, 10″, collection of Mr.and Mrs. Gerry Philpot.

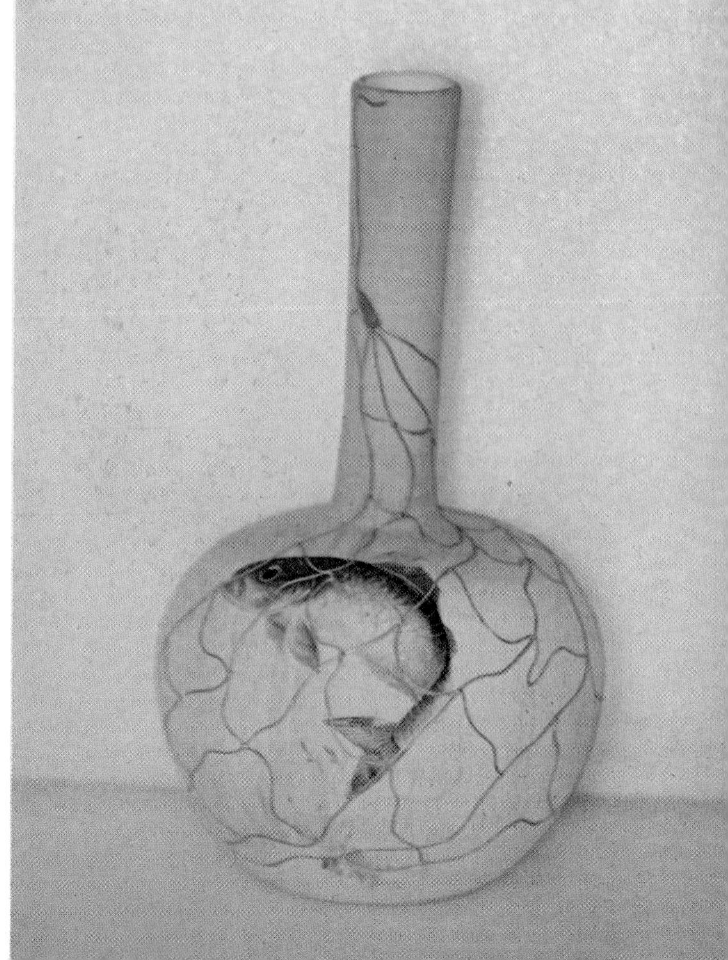

110. Wave Crest covered box with clock set in top, C. F. Monroe Company, signed *C.F.M. Co.*, 6″, collection of Mr. and Mrs. M. Michael Pearson.

111. Nakara covered box, C. F. Monroe Company, signed *Nakara,* 5 1/2″, collection of Dr. and Mrs. Alick Osofsky.

Text on p. 58

112. Wave Crest vase, C. F. Monroe Company, signed *Wave Crest, Trademark,* 4 1/2″ collection of Mr. and Mrs. Raymond Suppes.

113. Kelva covered box, C. F. Monroe Company, signed *Kelva,* 5 1/2″, chrysler Art Museum.

Text on p. 58

114. Vase, signed in script *Smith Bros.*, 8 3/4″, collection of Mr. and Mrs. Gerry Philpot.

115. Vase, Smith Brothers, signed with *a rampant lion in a shield and the words "trade mark,"* 8 1/2″, collection of Dr. and Mrs. Alick Osofsky.

116. Santa Maria ship decorated vase, Smith Brothers, signed copyright by *A. E. Smith,* 8 1/2″, collection of Mr. and Mrs. J. Michael Pearson.

Text on p. 58

117. Coralene Mother of Pearl vase with flower and spray beading, 6 1/4″, collection of Sally A. Rose.

118. Coralene Burmese vase, 6 3/4″, collection of Mrs. Matt T. Donahue.

119. Coralene on satin finish vase, 7″, collection of Mr. and Mrs. Raymond Suppes.

Text on p. 75

120. Coralene on satin finish basket, 7″, collection of Sally A. Rose.

121. Coralene Mother of Pearl vase, 8″, collection of Maude B. Feld.

Text on p. 75

122. Stevens and Williams decorated overlay vase, signed *Stevens and Williams, Art Glass, Stourbridge,* 7″, Rockwell Gallery.

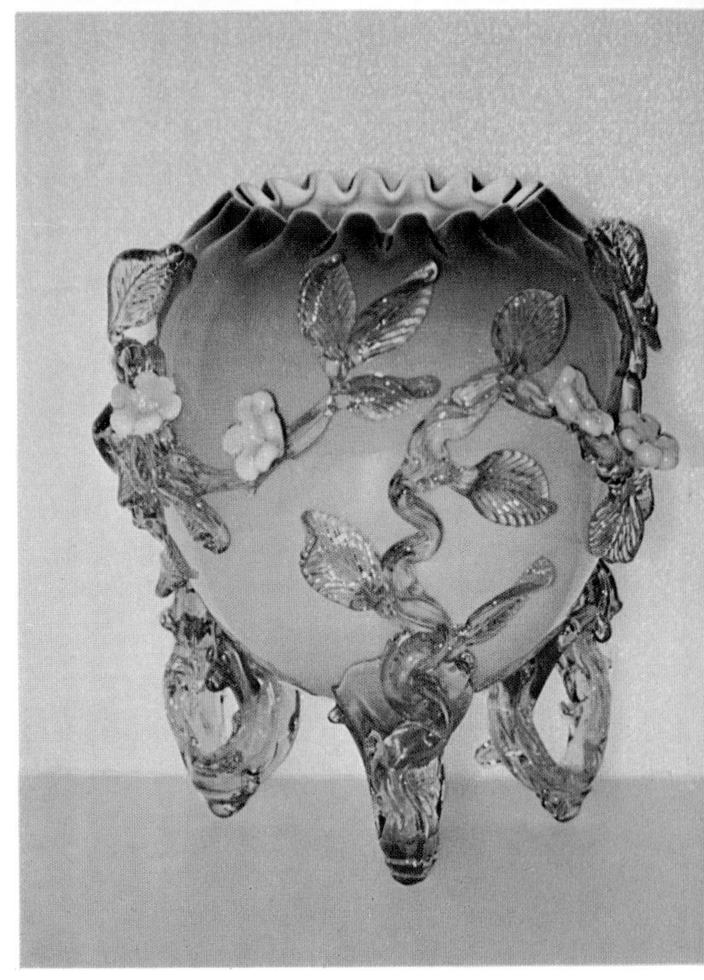

123. Pine cone overlay decorated vase, 9 1/2″, collection of Mr. and Mrs. Gerry Philpot.

124. Strawberry overlay decorated vase, 11″, Chrysler Art Museum.

Text on p. 75

on many utilitarian type wares including powder boxes, cookie jars, tobacco jars, and the like.

Smith Brothers (continued)

Plate 115 shows a covered jar with a chrysanthemum decoration that is similar to those found on many Crown Milano pieces offered by the Mt. Washington Glass Company. This is, of course, not surprising when it is borne in mind that the plants were neighbors and that both firms at one time or another undoubtedly employed many of the same artists.

Good taste was used in the selection of pieces for decoration. While we rarely come across an identifiable Smith Brothers lamp shade, it should be mentioned that they were one of the largest distributors of this decorated item in the United States.

* * * * *

Coralene

Plates pp. 72–73

Tiny pieces of colored glass placed upon the outer surface of the ware and then secured by firing make an easy identification for the glass named Coralene. Decorations may take the shape of underwater live coral, but may also be in a fleur-de-lis, herringbone, sheaf of wheat, or in fact any pattern which the artist designed and used. This glass bead decoration is found in all colors and on all types of glass, but is most sought after on pieces of Mother of Pearl. An unusual combination is shown in Plate 118 where the Coralene was applied to a Burmese vase. It should be remembered that Coralene beading is only a surface decoration, and indicates nothing else.

Use of this Coralene decoration was not restricted to any factory, American or foreign. It is most pleasing to the eye in a subdued or indirect light, seeming to give a phosphorescent or underwater effect with a luminous glow.

* * * * *

Overlay

Plates pp. 74, 76

Overlay, or applied glass decorating, is what the name implies: the method of embellishing vases, bowls, and other decorative articles with individual pieces of colored glass. Attributions are rashly made as to the very specific origin of many of the more striking pieces. We have noticed, however, that claims for the source of manufacture seemingly vary, reflecting the section of the country in which the pieces are found.

It should not be forgotten that from 1880 on, when production was prolific, there were adequate means of travel and transportation. Many of these types of overlay decorative work are attributed to the Hobbs, Brockunier Co., Wheeling, West Virginia, the Boston & Sandwich Glass Company, Sandwich, Massachusetts, as well as the Mt. Washington Glass Company, New Bedford, Massachusetts. We do know without question that this style of art glass was produced in England, particularly at Stevens & Williams, in view of the fact that a number of their

Text cont. on p. 78

125. Trumpet flower overlay decorated bowl, 5 1/2″, Chrysler Art Museum.

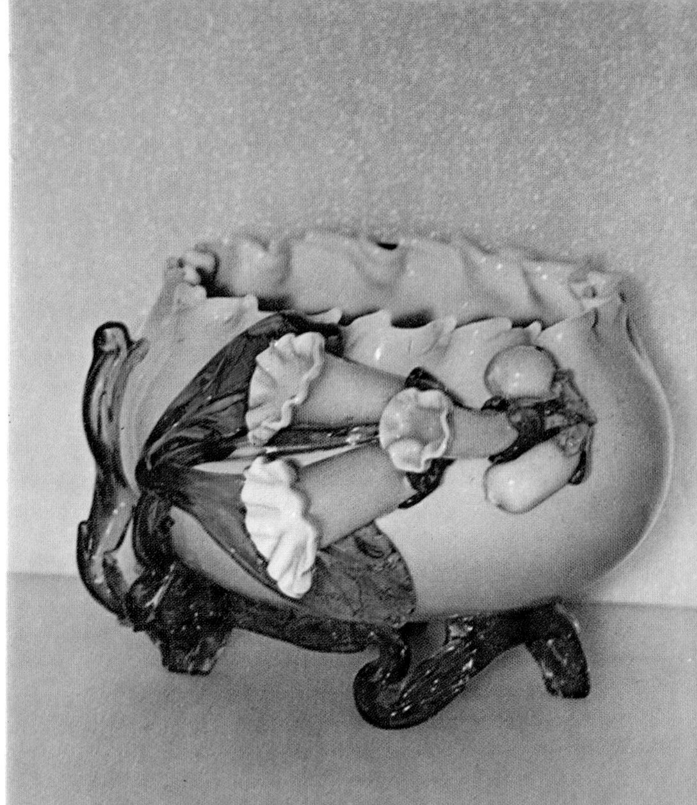

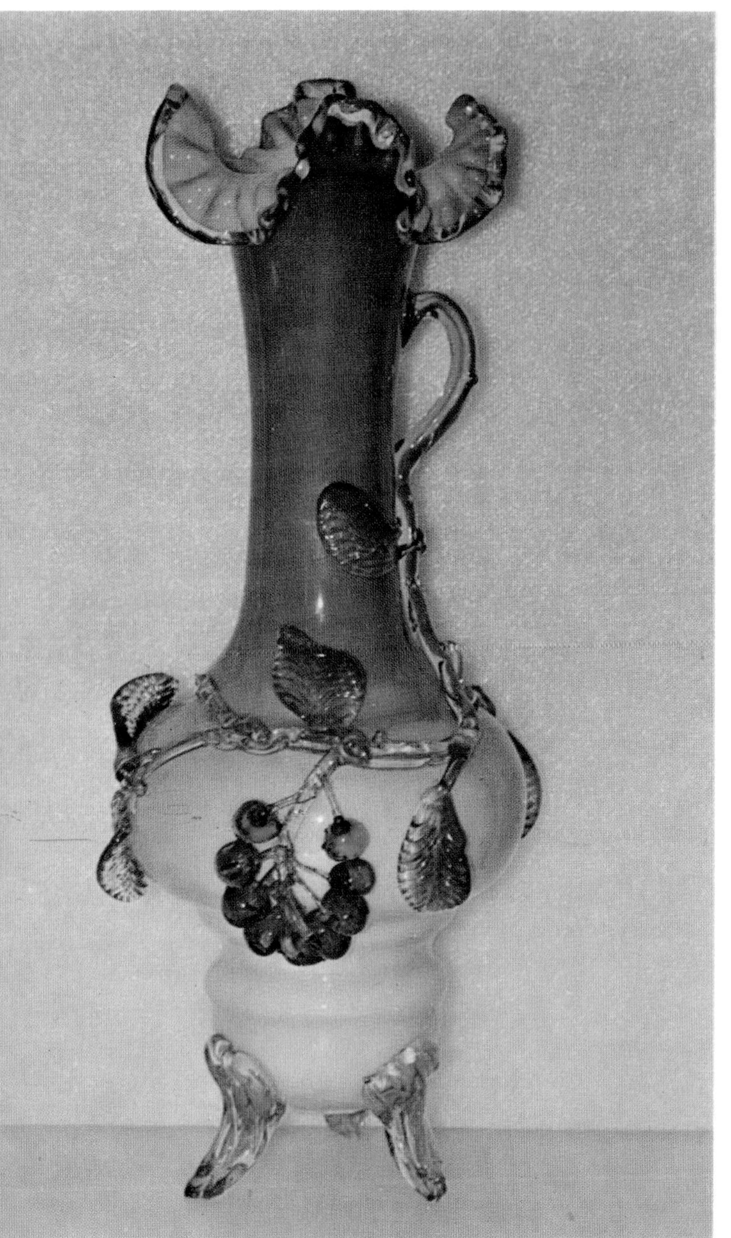

126. Overlay vase, 17″, collection of Mr. and Mrs. Gerry Philpot.

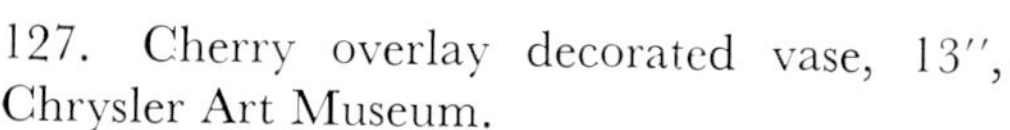

127. Cherry overlay decorated vase, 13″, Chrysler Art Museum.

Text on p. 75

128. Mary Gregory overlay vase with girl and butterfly net enamelling, attributed to the Boston & Sandwich Glass Co., Milan Historical Museum.

129. Mary Gregory Rubina Verde (red to green) vase with boy and butterfly net enamelling, attributed to the Boston &Sandwich Glass Co.,Milan Historical Museum.

Text on pp. 78–79

pieces had their mark impressed in the under part of the piece (Plate 122).

Overlay (continued)

Flowers and fruits were some of the most handsome and attractive applications used. Artistic concepts in glass are remarkably true to life. We have selected the illustrated pieces because good taste is reflected in balancing the decoration with the overall size and shape of the individual work.

Most of the overlays appear in a glossy finish, but this does not imply that acid finishing was not used. Without being repetitious, it may be seen in the examples shown what a large field the artist-workman had to choose from, and that certainly one of the outstanding traits of art glass designers was originality.

* * * * *

Boston & Sandwich Glass Company

Plates pp. 77, 80–81

The quiet, Cape Cod town of Sandwich, Massachusetts, was the site of one of the older American glass factories, the Boston & Sandwich Glass Company. Known primarily for their pressed glasswares from the early 1830's, they ultimately produced a large range of novelty art glass.

Unfortunately there is a lack of signed work from this noted factory. There are, however, many interested collectors who dig in the refuse dump of the factory in an effort to salvage shards or pieces that may be useful for identification purposes. In addition, the fine museum devoted primarily to Sandwich glass, located in the town of Sandwich and invitingly open to the public, has many displays of their own as well as permanent loan collections. This museum also has several cases of interesting shards recovered from the factory dump that are matched up to pieces on display.

Painted Amberina (Plate 133) was made in 1870. Shards of similar wares are in the Museum, with matching hobs. This particular type of amberina is also seen in the pink to white hobnail pattern. Instead of the colors being inherently a part of the glass itself, they are in fact stains applied to the outer surface, and then refired to set the colors. When held up to the light, stain effects similar to that of clothing stains may be noticed where there was a slight running of the liquid color when application was made. The pitcher shown has a known history from the time it was secured from Sandwich as a wedding gift in 1870 to the present time. Ten punch cups formed an addition to this set.

Mary Gregory glass (Plates 128 and 129), named after the decorator, is believed to be the original work of the Boston & Sandwich Glass Company because of the glass itself, and the fine enameling depicts young children engaged in butterfly collecting. There are also other known Mary Gregory subjects, but it should be realized that only an extremely small percentage of the so-called Mary Gregory pieces on the market today were every produced at Sandwich. Most of the children originally pictured in enamels were in the under-twelve-years-of-age group. An additional indication of an original Mary Gregory piece is the finished detail of the complete subject, including the children's facial features.

Icicle glass, Plate 132, is attributed to Sandwich and is in effect a construction of icicle type overlays dripping down from the rim of the piece.

Fireglow, see Plate 134 and Plate 136, is attributed to Sandwich. At first glance there is a great similarity to English Bristol type glass. Pieces should be held up to the light, peering through the top of the article to the foot. A reddish brown color of varying intensity will probably be quite noticeable. Pieces are generally in a light acid finish and frequently decorated. European glassmakers made similar ware but the Sandwich productions seem to have a particular tannish surface cast all their own.

Tortoise-Shell glass, as shown in Plates 130 and 131, may or may not be of Sandwich origin because a number of European makers also turned out very fine work in this medium, including similar shapes. The ware has a glossy finish, and the brown mottling is between the two layers of glass. Value of individual pieces lies in the overall quality of the article itself rather than its origin.

* * * * *

Cut Velvet

Plate p. 81

Cut Velvet is the name commonly used in referring to pieces similar in pattern to that shown in Plate 135. Constructed of two laminated layers of glass with the inner casing frequently in white, this type of ware was blown into a mold to develop the required pattern. In this particular example it is diamond shaped, raised slightly from the outer surface. Except on rare occasions, it is acid finished or velvet in texture. Other patterns are common, as are various shapes and colors.

Quality of the overall piece would determine its desirability, inasmuch as many factories turned out this type of ware in the United States and elsewhere.

* * * * *

Tiffany

Plates pp. 83 ff.

Louis Comfort Tiffany, 1848–1934, developed a unique type of glass in the art field. We arbitrarily divide his glass into two categories: commercial and art pieces. In the commercial group we include sets of dinnerware such as cups, saucers, plates, wines, sherbets, goblets, and tumblers. This group is not pictured in the book, but rather do we stress the special glass pieces that reflect individual effort.

Uniqueness is common to Tiffany, for we note that in addition to

Text cont. on p. 82

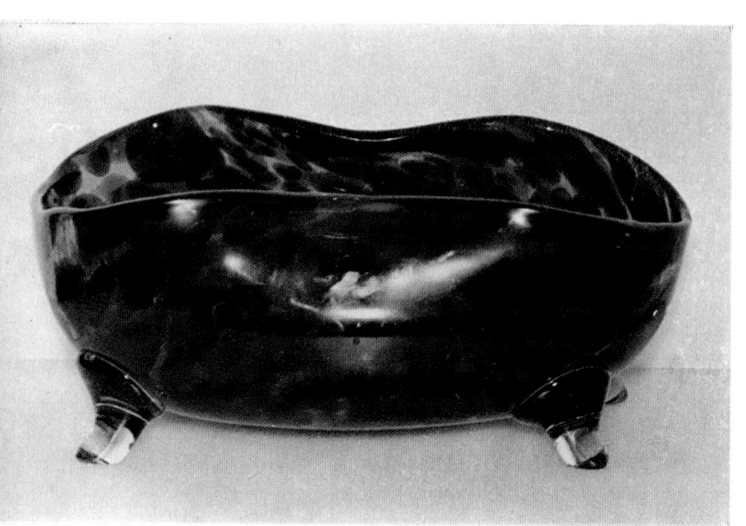

130. Tortoise Shell footed bowl, attributed to the Boston & Sandwich Glass Co., 4 1/2″, Chrysler Art Museum.

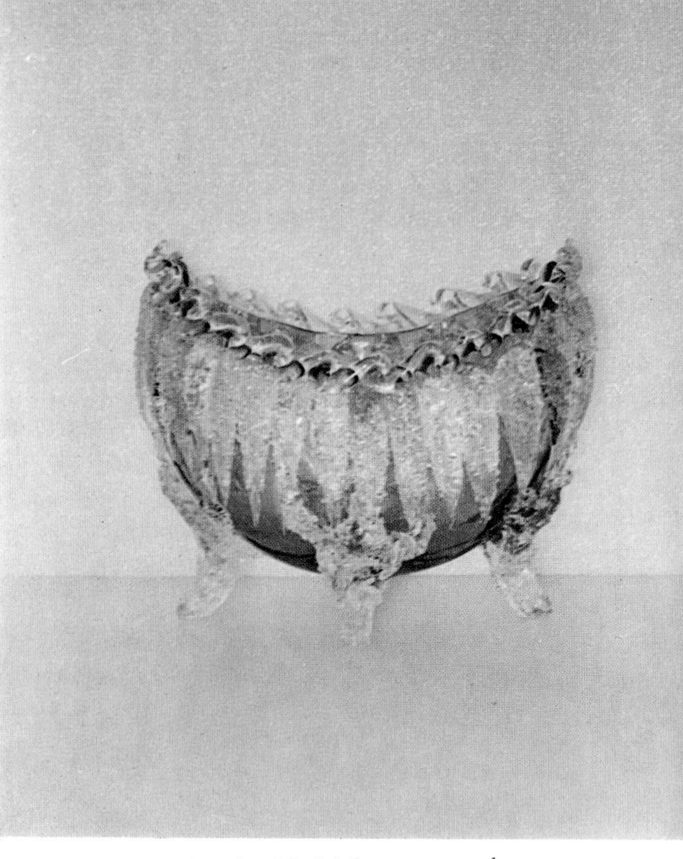

132. Icicle glass bowl with icicle type overlay application, rigaree overlay on rim, attributed to the Boston & Sandwich Glass Co., 4 3/4″, Milan Historical Museum.

131. Tortoise Shell pitcher, attributed to the Boston & Sandwich Glass Co., 13 1/2″, collection of Mr. and Mrs. Raymond Suppes.

133. Painted Amberina pitcher, produced in 1870 by the Boston & Sandwich Glass Co., 7″, authors' collection.

Text on pp. 78–79

134. Fireglow covered rose jar with insert, attributed to the Boston & Sandwich Glass Co., 5 1/2″, Milan Historical Museum.

135. Cut Velvet stick vase with diamond quilting on a cased white bowl of glass, Boston & Sandwich Glass Co., 10 3/4″, collection of Mr. and Mrs. C. W. Bray.

136. Fireglow vase, attributed to the Boston & Sandwich Glass Co., 9 1/4″, collection of Mr. and Mrs. Gerry Philpot.

Text on p. 79

colors found in other art glass, Tiffany was able to project movement in form and shape in his work.

Tiffany (continued)

Structurally, Tiffany is found in single as well as multiple-layered glass. It comes transparent, translucent, as well as opaque. Every color in the rainbow will be found to have been used as well as an unlimited number of combinations.

For identification we roughly group the ware as follows, bearing in mind that any given type quite possibly could be combined with another. In approximate order of their rarity of color, but not necessarily of beauty, we find gold to be the most common, then blue, green, white, yellow, brown, amethyst, black, and red. There is also a whole group of the above colors in pastel shades, occuring in the same order of scarcity.

Plates pp. 87 ff.

Group 1: Single-color iridescent pieces. In effect, iridescent glass is produced when the surface of the glass is broken up into many thousands of fractures, which in turn breaks up the rays of light reflected to our eyes into a multitude of colors, although usually of one predominant shade.

Group 2: Decorated iridescent glass. The decorations are usually colored fibres of glass layed on the original piece and hooked with metal wires to form a design on the original piece, and then the two or more layers of glass are rolled on the working board, or marver, until there is a single layer of glass with the decoration already worked in. Shapes may also be developed to complement these decorations. Plates pp. 84 ff. Included in this latter group would be flower forms such as bulbous tulips or lily tops on long stems with wide bases. These are normally about seventeen inches high.

Plates p. 95

Group 3: Millefiore pieces. In these pieces long millefiore canes are sliced very thin, then imbedded in the outer surface, and the work rolled on the marver until there is a smooth outer surface. This is developed into beautiful floral patterns. It should be noted that Tiffany was always partial to natural floral effects.

Plates pp. 96 ff.

Group 4: Paperweight type. These are probably the rarest and most sought after: the very ultimate in glass beauty. Structurally we might describe the technique as that of having the colored decorative glass designs layed upon and imbedded in the inner layer of glass, with another layer of glass being then coated over the original decorated piece. The outer layer of glass would then frequently be treated to enable the finished piece to be slightly iridescent. This iridescence is also frequently found on the inner lining, but should not be confused with discoloration occasioned by leaving flowers stand in the same water level too long. In addition we have seen engraved patterns cut into the outer layer, giving very striking depth to the piece. Floral and under-

Text cont. on p. 116

137. Blue pastel Tiffany vase, signed *L.C.T. Favrile, 1821, 7″*, collection of Helen Eisenberg.

138. Yellow pastel Tiffany vase, signed *L. C. Tiffany Favrile, 1938,* 5 3/4″, collection of Mr. and Mrs. Hugh McKean.

139. Pink pastel Tiffany tazza, signed *L. C. T. Favrile, 7″*, collection of Helen Eisenberg.

Text on p. 82

140. Flower-form Tiffany vase, signed *L.C.T. M 2068,* 13 1/2″, collection of Mr. and Mrs. Hugh McKean.

141. Flower-form Tiffany vase, signed *L.C.T. M 525–1,* 13″, collection of Mr. and Mrs. Hugh McKean.

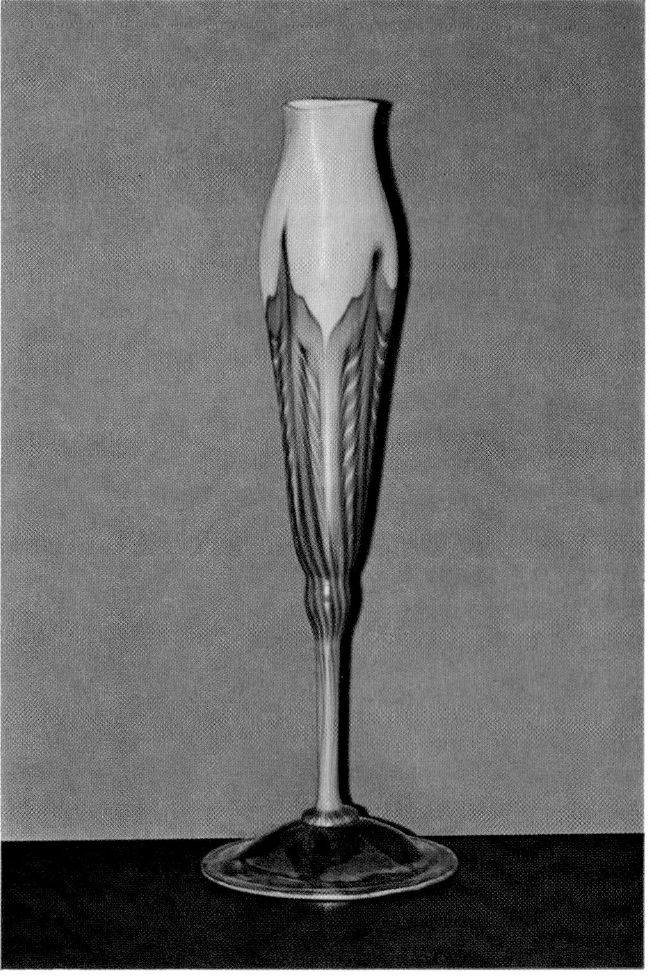

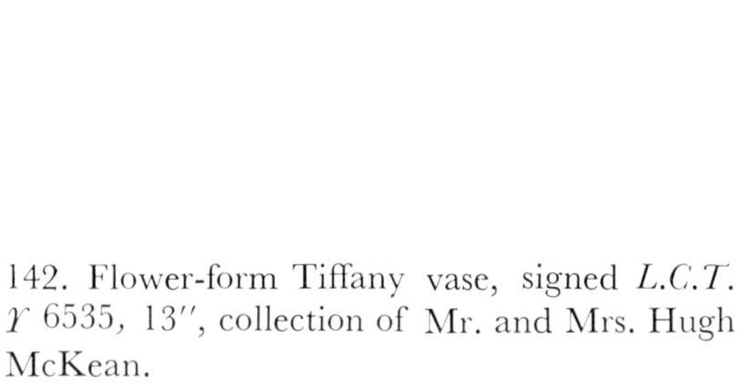

142. Flower-form Tiffany vase, signed *L.C.T. Y 6535,* 13″, collection of Mr. and Mrs. Hugh McKean.

Text on p. 82

143 Iridescent gold, Jack-in-the--pulpit Tiffany vase, signed *L. C. Tiffany, Favrile* 3918 *G,* 19″, collection of Mr. and Mrs. Hugh McKean.

144. Flower-form Tiffany vase, signed *L. C. T.,* 14 1/4″.

Text on p. 82

145. Flower-form Tiffany vase with cameo decoration, signed *L.C.T. W 6810,* 13 3/4″, collection of Helen Eisenberg. (left)

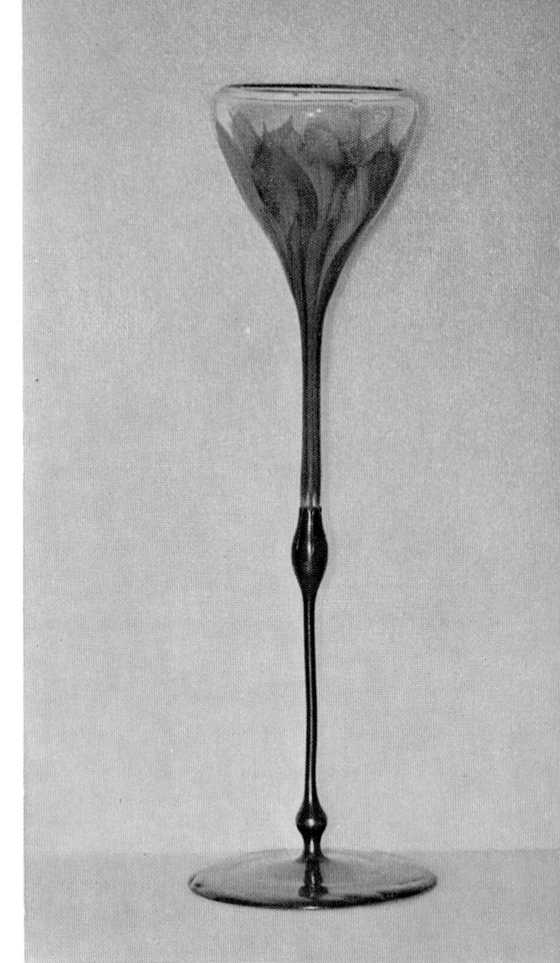

146. Flower-form Tiffany vase, signed *L.C.T. -U 5324,* metal holder signed *Tiffany Studios, N.Y.,* 18″, collection of J. Jonathon Joseph. (right)

147. Flower-form Tiffany vase, signed *L.C.T. T 691,* 18 1/4″, collection of Mr. and Mrs. J. Michael Pearson. (left)

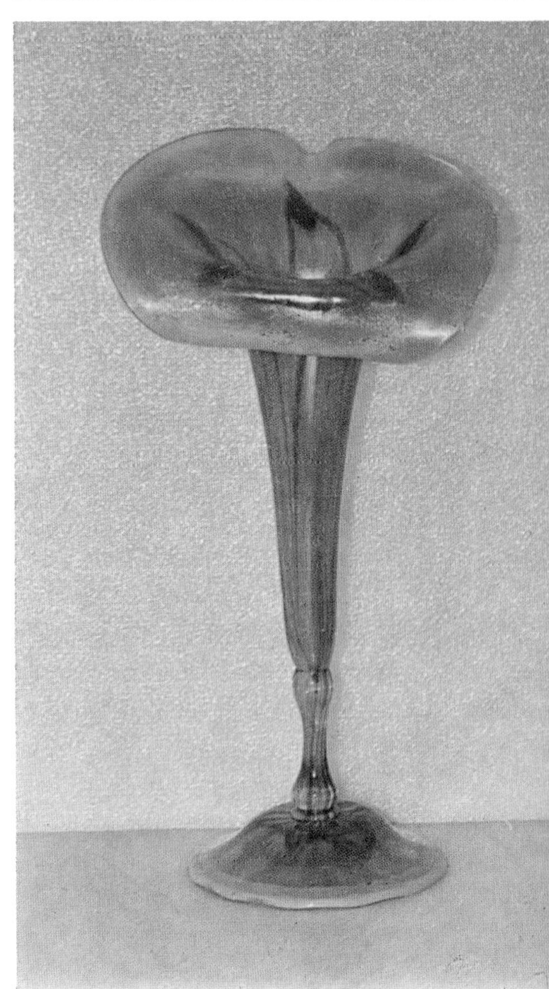

148. Flower-form Tiffany vase, signed *L.C.T. M 5284,* 14 1/2″, collection of Mr. and Mrs. J. Michael Pearson. (right)

Text on p. 82

149. Iridescent red and gold Tiffany vase, signed *L. C. T. E 1813,* 11″, collection of Helen Eisenberg.

Text on p. 82

150. Brown iridescent Tiffany vase, signed *L.C.T. 9459 A*, 8 1/2″, collection of Maude B. Feld.

151. Brown iridescent gourd-shaped Tiffany vase, signed *L. C. Tiffany, Favrile, E 1794*, 10 1/4″, collection of Lillian Nassau.

152. Iridescent triple gourd-shaped Tiffany vase, signed *Louis C. Tiffany 07118*, 9″, collection of J. Jonathon Joseph.

153. Brown iridescent gourd-shaped Tiffany vase, signed *L. C. Tiffany, Favrile, 3222 H*, 11″, collection of Mr. and Mrs. Bernard Berger.

Text on p. 82

154. Blue iridescent Tiffany vase, free form, signed *L.C.T. W 5810,* 6″, collection of Mr. and Mrs. Milton Collin.

155. Blue iridescent Tiffany vase, signed *L. C. Tiffany, Favrile 5651 G,* 18 1/4″, collection of Dr. and Mrs. Walter Donahue.

Text on p. 82

156. Green and black iridescent Tiffany vase, signed *L. C. Tiffany, Favrile,* 8″, collection of Mr. and Mrs. Joseph Favorito.

157. Iridescent Tiffany chalice, signed *L. C. Tiffany, Favrile Y 8918,* 10 3/4″, collection of Helen Eisenberg.

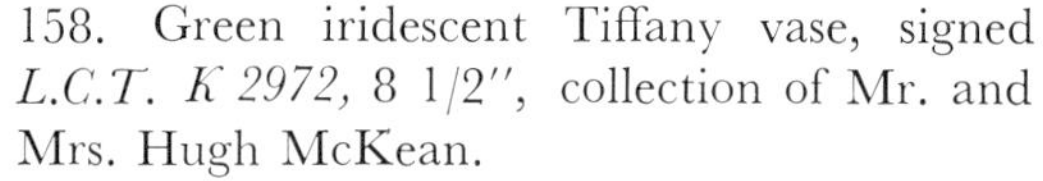

158. Green iridescent Tiffany vase, signed *L.C.T. K 2972,* 8 1/2″, collection of Mr. and Mrs. Hugh McKean.

Text on p. 82

159. Red iridescent Tiffany vase, signed *L. C. Tiffany, Favrile* 2191 *J*, 4 1/2″, collection of Mr. and Mrs. Hugh McKean.

160. Tiffany vase, signed *5934 E, L. C. Tiffany, Favrile,* 8 3/4″, Chrysler Art Museum.

161. Red, with green collar, iridescent Tiffany vase, signed *L. C. Tiffany, Favrile 5973 E,* 5 1/2″, collection of Mr. and Mrs. Hugh McKean.

Text on p. 82

162. Black iridescent Tiffany cologne bottle with matching numbered stopper, signed *L. C. T. D 1180,* 7 3/4″, collection of Helen Eisenberg.

163. Iridescent, gooseneck-shaped Tiffany vase, signed *L. C. T. 1156 A,* 13″, collection of Helen Eisenberg.

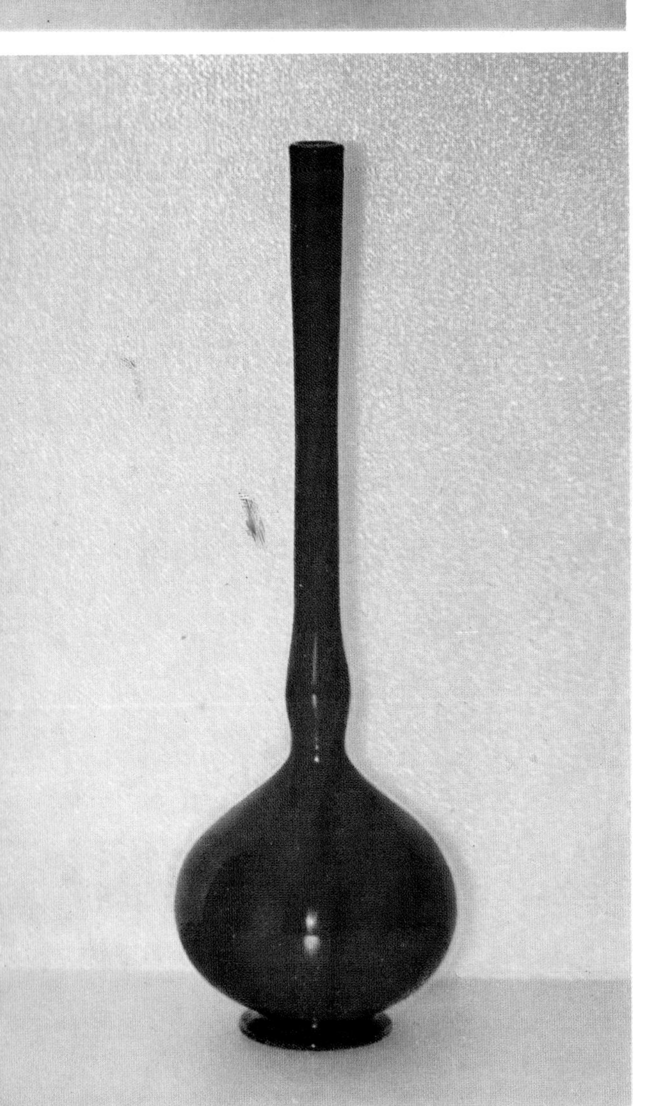

164. Red Tiffany vase, signed *L. C. Tiffany, Favrile 5593 E,* 12 1/2″, collection of J. Jonathon Joseph.

Text on p. 82

165. Blue satin iridescent Tiffany vase, signed *L. C. Tiffany, Favrile 1678 E,* 8 1/2″, collection of Mr. and Mrs. Hugh McKean.

166. Blue satin iridescent Tiffany vase, signed *L. C. Tiffany, Favrile* 8540 *M,* 6 1/4″, collection of Mr. and Mrs. Hugh McKean.

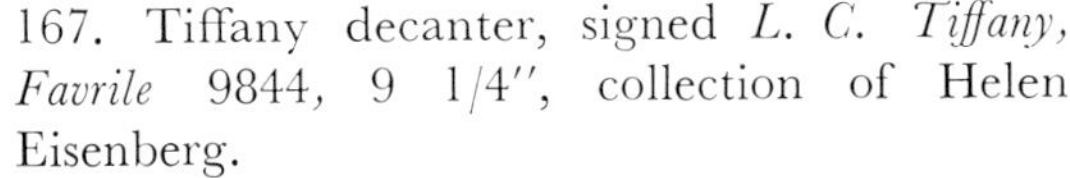

167. Tiffany decanter, signed *L. C. Tiffany, Favrile* 9844, 9 1/4″, collection of Helen Eisenberg.

168. Red and black iridescent Tiffany vase, signed *L. C. Tiffany Inc. Favrile 3990 N,* 6 1/2″, collection of Mr. and Mrs. Hugh McKean.

Text on p. 82

169. Blue iridescent Tiffany vase, signed *L. C. T. N 404,* 4″, collection of Maude B. Feld.

170. Blue decorated black iridescent Tiffany vase, signed *L. C. Tiffany, Favrile 8283 J*, 5 1/4″, collection of Mrs. Matt T. Donahue.

171. Iridescent Tiffany vase, signed *L. C. Tiffany, Favrile 9595,* 4 1/4″, collection of Helen Eisenberg.

Text on p. 82

172. Gold millefiore iridescent Tiffany vase, signed *L. C. Tiffany, Favrile D 752, San Francisco,* 5″, collection of Dr. and Mrs. Walter Donahue.

173. Iridescent millefiore Tiffany vase, signed 1553 *B*, 7 1/2″, collection of Mr. and Mrs. Hugh McKean.

174. Iridescent millefiore Tiffany vase, signed *Louis C. Tiffany, R 4017,* 11″, collection of Mr. and Mrs. Hugh McKean.

Text on p. 82

175. Paperweight Tiffany vase, signed *L. C. Tiffany Favrile 3685 P,* 7 1/4″, collection of Helen Eisenberg.

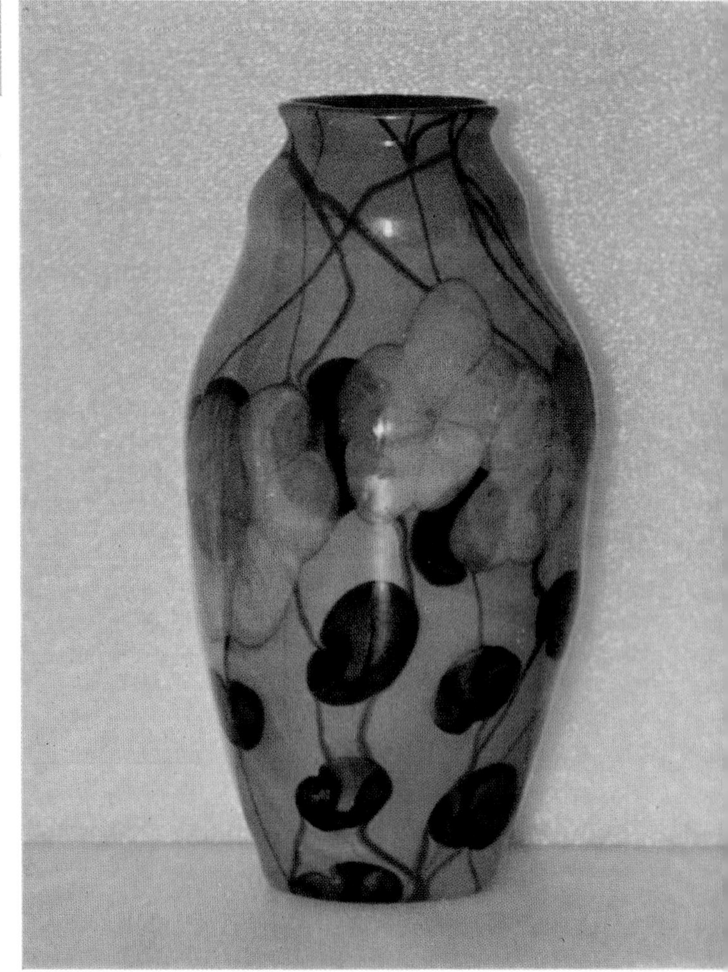

176. Paperweight Tiffany vase, signed *L. C. T. 6683 B,* 8 1/4″, collection of Helen Eisenberg.

Text on p. 82

177. Morning-glory paperweight Tiffany vase, signed *L. S. T. W 7387*, 8″, collection of J. Jonathon Joseph.

Text on p. 82

178. Gladioli paperweight Tiffany vase, signed *L. C. Tiffany, Favrile, Exhibition Piece 256 J*, 12″, collection of J. Jonathon Joseph.

179. Paperweight, narcissus design Tiffany vase, signed *L. C. Tiffany, Favrile 3270 G*, 4″, collection of J. Jonathon Joseph.

180. Marine paperweight Tiffany vase, signed *L. C. Tiffany, Favrile*, 5194 *G*, 4 3/4″, Corning Museum of Glass.

Text on p. 82

181. Marine paperweight Tiffany vase, 5″, collection of Maude B. Feld.

182. Paperweight Tiffany vase, signed *Louis C. Tiffany, Furnaces, Inc. 831 N,* 14″, Chrysler Art Museum.

183. Aquamarine paperweight Tiffany vase, signed *L. C. Tiffany Inc. Favrile, Panama Pcific Ex. 5399 M,* 12″, collection of Mr. and Mrs. Hugh McKean.

Text on p. 82

184. Paperweight Tiffany vase with crocus design, signed *L.C.T. T 1838,* 4 1/2″, collection of Helen Eisenberg.

185. Red paperweight Tiffany vase, signed *L. C. Tiffany, Favrile 9452 H,* 8″, collection of J. Jonathon Joseph.

Text on p. 82

186. Paperweight Tiffany vase, signed in metal base *Tiffany Co., N.Y.*, 16 1/2″, collection of Dr. and Mrs. Walter Donahue.

Text on p. 82

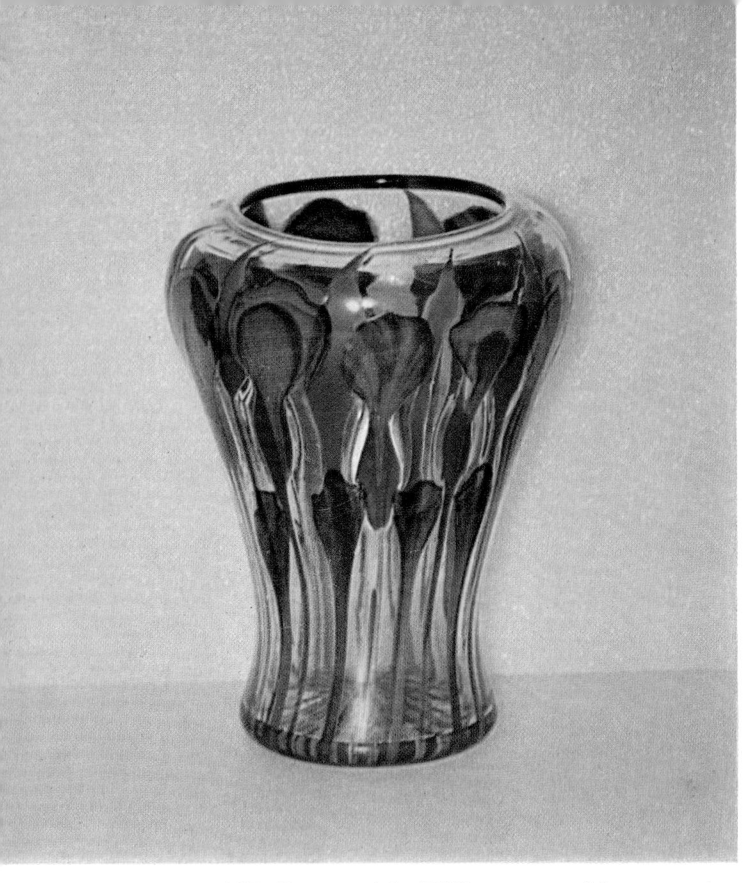

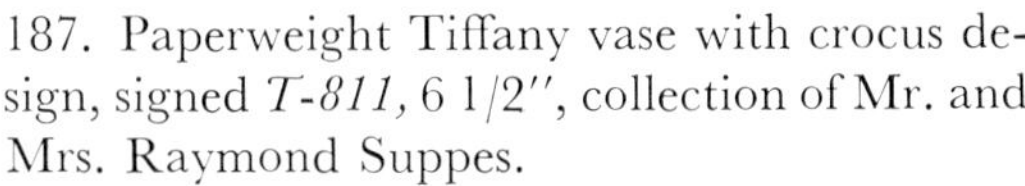

187. Paperweight Tiffany vase with crocus design, signed *T-811,* 6 1/2″, collection of Mr. and Mrs. Raymond Suppes.

188. Paperweight Tiffany vase, signed *L. C. Tiffany, Favrile 9136 C,* 7″, collection of Mrs. Matt T. Donahue.

189. Paperweight Tiffany vase with iridescent gold liner suspended from the inner top of the vase, signed *L. C. T. Y 3127,* 5 1/2″, collection of Mr. and Mrs. Raymond Suppes.

190. Poppy paperweight Tiffany vase, signed *L. C. Tiffany, Favrile, 2808 G,* 8″, private collection.

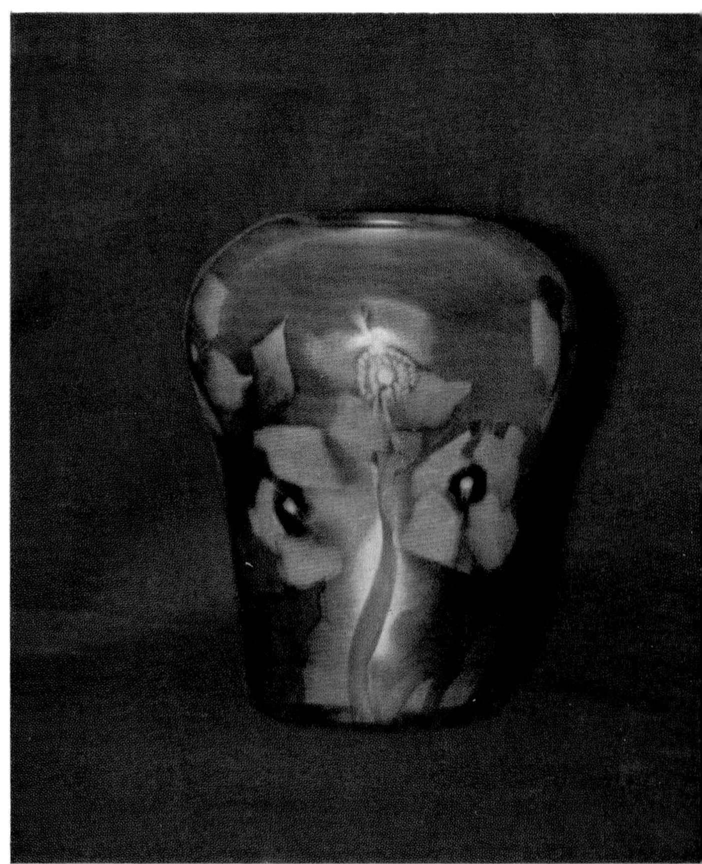

Text on p. 82

191. Tiffany iridescent gold Cypriote vase, signed *Louis C. Tiffany, L. C. T. 1771,* 7 1/2″, collection of Mr. and Mrs. Hugh McKean.

192. Tiffany iridescent Cypriote vase, signed *L. C. Tiffany Inc. Favrile 4374 N,* 9 1/2″, collection of Lillian Nassau.

Text on p. 116

193. Tiffany iridescent blue Cypriote vase, signed *L. C. Tiffany, Favrile 7264 J,7″*, collection of J. Jonathon Joseph.

194. Tiffany black iridescent Cypriote vase, signed *L.C.T. 482 Q*, 7 1/2″, Chrysler Museum of Art.

195. Tiffany Cypriote paperweight vase, signed *L. C. Tiffany, Favrile 51 A. Coll.*, 6 3/4″, collection of J. Jonathon Joseph.

Text on p. 116

196. Iridescent Lava Tiffany vase, signed *L. C. Tiffany, Favrile, 6573 N,* 6 1/2″, collection of Helen Eisenberg.

Text on p. 116

197. Lava Tiffany vase, 4 1/2″, collection of Mr. and Mrs. Raymond Suppes.

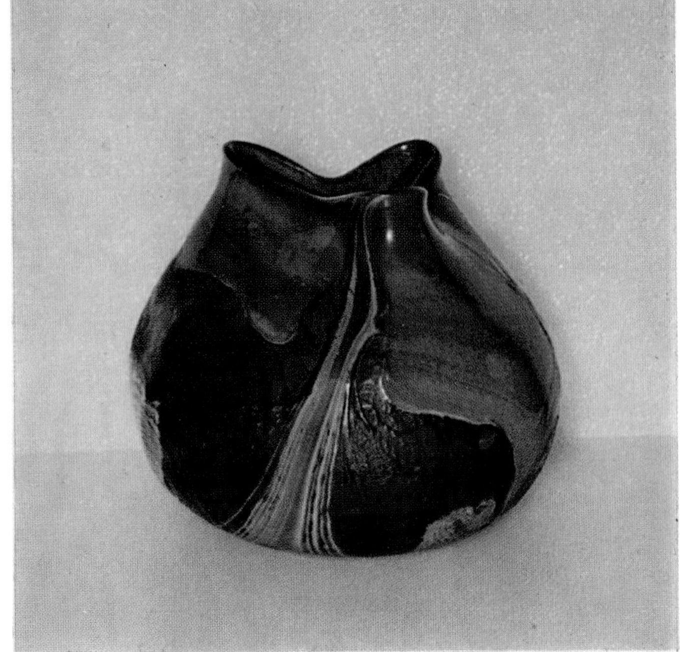

198. Iridescent Lava Tiffany vase with peacock feather design, signed *L. C. Tiffany Inc. Favrile 9590 M*, 5 1/4″, Chrysler Art Museum.

199. Iridescent Lava Tiffany vase, signed *L. C. Tiffany, 347 J*, 5 1/4″, collection of Helen Eisenberg.

Text on p. 116

200. Iridescent Lava Tiffany vase, signed *L. C. Tiffany, Favrile 4075 C,* 6 1/2″, collection of Helen Eisenberg.

201. Iridescent Lava Tiffany vase, signed *L. C. Tiffany, Favrile 1773 B,* 6 1/2″, collection of Lillian Nassau.

Text on p. 116

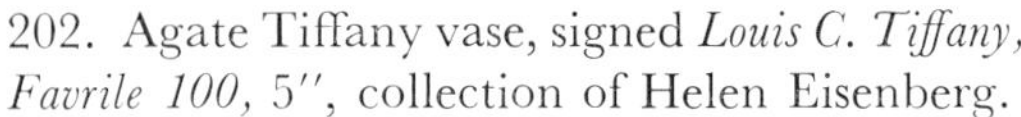

202. Agate Tiffany vase, signed *Louis C. Tiffany, Favrile 100,* 5″, collection of Helen Eisenberg.

203. Agate Tiffany vase, signed *Louis C. Tiffany 07211,* 8 1/2″, Chrysler Art Museum.

204. Agate Tiffany vase, signed, *L. C. Tiffany, Favrile 7176 J,* 6″, collection of Lillian Nassau.

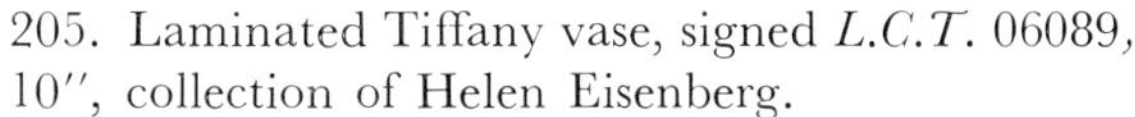

205. Laminated Tiffany vase, signed *L.C.T.* 06089, 10″, collection of Helen Eisenberg.

Text on p. 116

206. Marbleized, brick color Tiffany vase, signed *L. C. T. 1460,* 5″, collection of Mr. and Mrs. Hugh McKean.

Text on p. 116

207. Paperweight, cameo and intaglio combination Tiffany vase, signed *Louis C. Tiffany 06767, Favrile,* 4 1/4″, private collection.

208. Tiffany cameo vase, signed *L. C. Tiffany, Favrile 4212 A,* 5 3/4″, collection of Helen Eisenberg

209. Tiffany cameo vase, signed *L. C. Tiffany, 1647 C,* 8″, collection of Helen Eisenberg.

210. Iridescent cameo Tiffany vase with peacock in relief, signed *L. C. Tiffany, Favrile 01935,* 8 1/4″, collection of Helen Eisenberg.

Text on p. 116

211. Intaglio cut, iridescent Tiffany bowl, signed *L. C. Tiffany, Favrile, Q*, 9 1/2″, collection of Frances D. Armentrout.

212. Intaglio cut Tiffany vase, signed *T & C* monogram, 6 3/4″, collection of Mr. and Mrs. Hugh McKean.

213. Intaglio cut, iridescent Tiffany vase, signed *L. C. Tiffany, Favrile 3639 K*, 16″, collection of Mr. and Mrs. *F. M.* Holland.

214. Intaglio cut Tiffany vase, signed *L. C. Tiffany, Favrile, 4267 A, Panama Pacific Ex.*, 11 1/2″, collection of Helen Eisenberg.

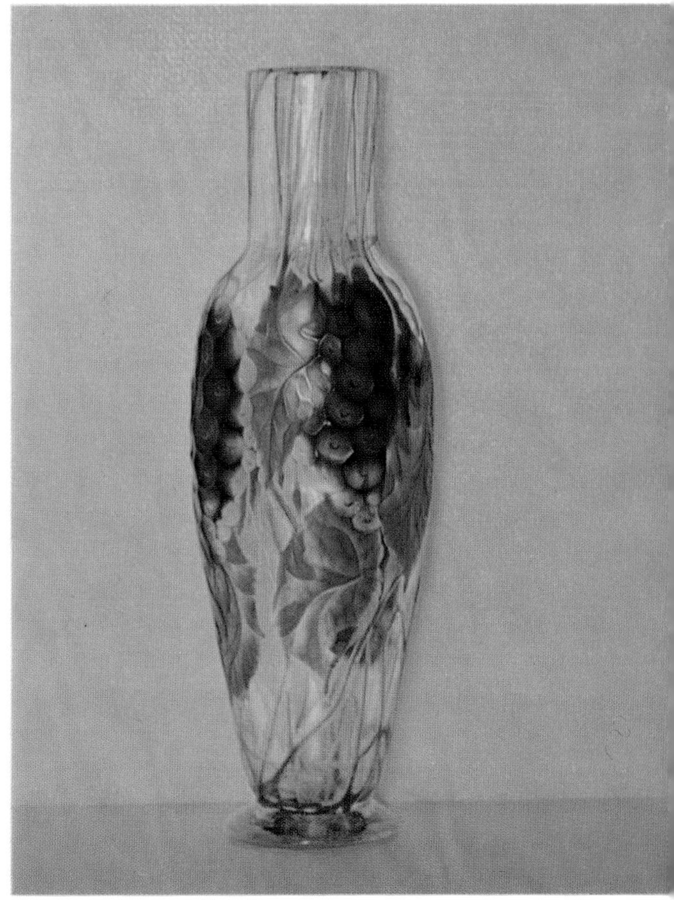

Text on p. 116

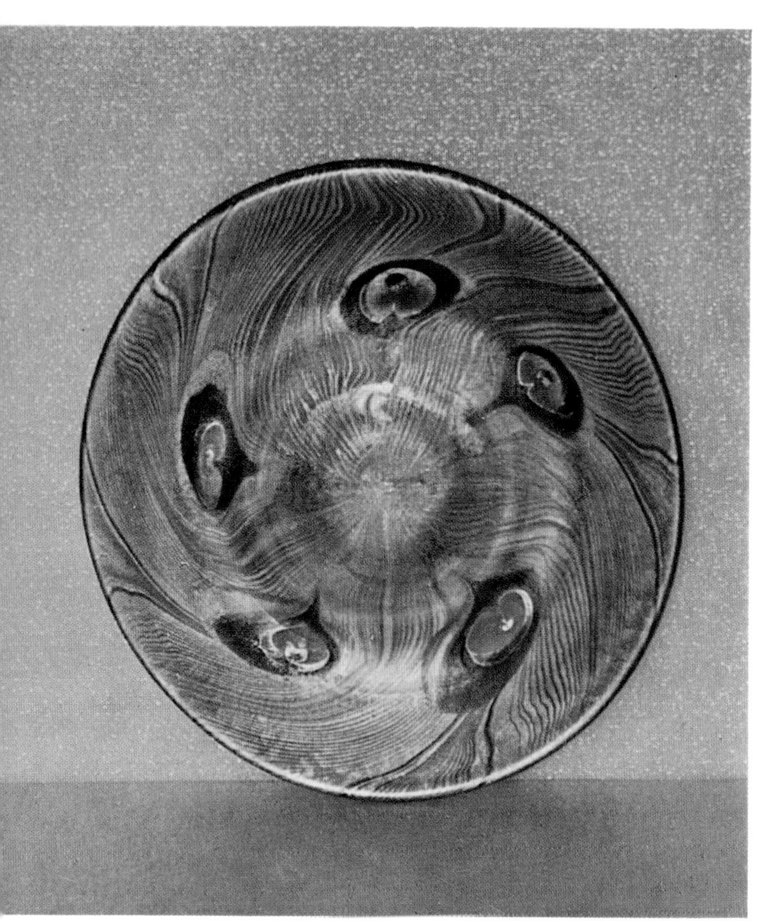

215. Iridescent peacock feather Tiffany plate, signed *L. C. T. K 2423,* 6 1/4″, collection of Dr. and Mrs. Alick Osofsky.

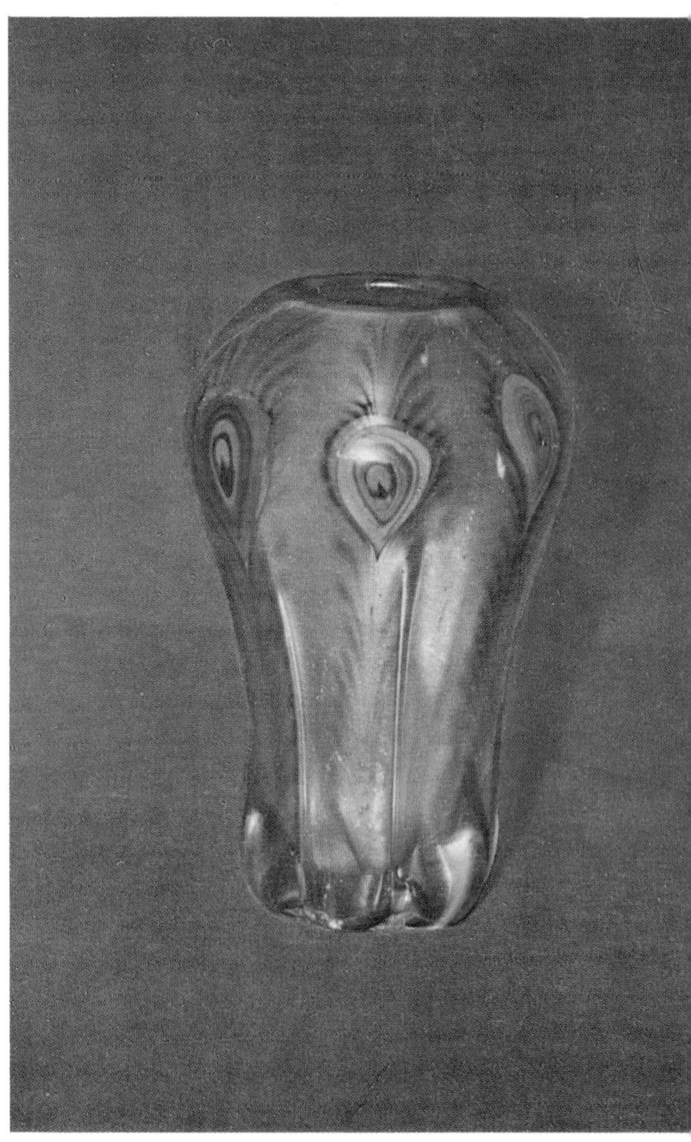

216. Paperweight peacock feather Tiffany vase, signed *Louis C. Tiffany, Inc., Exhibition piece, 7400 N,* 7″, Chrysler Art Museum.

Text on p. 116

217. Diatreta, iridescent blue Tiffany tazza, signed *L. C. Tiffany, Favrile, 6207 D*, 8″, Chrysler Art Museum.

Text on pp. 116–117

218. Daffodil Tiffany lamp, signed *Tiffany Studios, New York,* 25″, Chrysler Art Museum.

219. Moorish mosaic Tiffany lamp, signed *Tiffany Studios, New York,* 17″, Chrysler Art Museum.

220. Tiffany lamp, signed *Tiffany Studios, New York,* 20″, collection of Mr. and Mrs. Barry Gerstein.

Text on pp. 116–117

221. Tiffany twelve branch lily lamp, signed *Tiffany Studios, New York,* 19 1/2″, Chrysler Art Museum.

Text on p. 117

water marine life predominate in the paperweight technique. Millefiore canes are flattened and spread out to become flowers such as morning glories, narcissus, daffodils, Queen Anne's lace, and a host of others.

Tiffany (continued)

Plates pp. 103-4 Group 5: Cypriote, or simulated buried glass of the old Roman times. Tans and blues are seen most frequently, with the surface best described as being constructed of groups of minute, burst bubbles, pinhead in size. This is done to resemble the results of oxidation, or decomposition of the surface of glass when buried in the ground. Earth seemingly hastened this ageing process in the ancient Roman glass.

Plates pp. 105 ff. Group 6: Lava Glass. This is found in unusually free form shapes. Quite often we find this ware in two-color, wide banded, spiral designs, the colors being deep blue and iridescent gold, with splotchy iridessent gold also found hit and miss on the deep blue. This type of ware can be extremely sinuous in shape, possibly only second to the paperweight group.

Plates p. 108 Group 7: Agate. This is made up of various layers of glass and then polished smooth so that a laminated effect is achieved, closely resembling polished agate stone.

Plate p. 109 Group 8: Marbleized ware. This is similar to the agate type, though not polished down to reveal laminations but rather finished with an irregular surface revealing the colored striations and veinings commonly found in natural marble.

Plates p. 110 Group 9: Cameo glass. Consisting of two or more layers, this glass is exposed to acid and when not protected by an acid resistant material covering the ultimate design, the outer layer of glass is eaten away revealing the under layer or layers. After the acid resistant material is removed, cutting and polishing tools are then used to shape and bring to life the originally intended outer surface decoration.

Plates p. 111 Group 10: Intaglio. This refers to the technique whereby designs are cut into or engraved in the outer surface. Contrasting colored glass is then placed in these engravings, and the cutting again resumed so that we have engraved work on decorative inlays. A number of these pieces have only an "O" prefixed to the numbers on the base, and without other markings such as L.C.T., or Favrile (literally interpreted to mean hand wrought).

Plates p. 112 Group 11: Peacock Feather. This is mentioned as a group only because it is one of the most effective designs that Tiffany used constantly on all types of his work. Colors and the shape of true peacock feathers are strikingly and quite faithfully reproduced on plainly applied outer surfaces or in paperweight vases, an example of which is shown in plate 216.

Plate p. 113 Group 12: Diatreta work. This is best described as a heavily constructed latticework applied at numerous points to the main body of the vase, but definitely an applied decoration, attached to but standing out from the original body. The openwork is usually diamond shaped.

Group 13. This includes the early green and amber, partially transparent, swirled bottle glass. These pieces, although frequently unmarked, are unquestionably Tiffany in view of the fact that Tiffany himself directly and through his company donated numerous pieces to leading museums where they may be viewed today. Using various museum pieces, signed or otherwise, as a guideline, you will soon come to recognize Tiffany shapes, color effects, and techniques of work.

Stained glass windows, mosaics, enamels, jewelry embodying iridescent glass, lamps with shades of floral and insect designs, are to be found in most museum collections having Tiffany glass. Plates pp. 114 ff.

You will note that in the plate descriptions we have indicated in italics all markings found on the various pieces, including the accompanying numerals. We make no indication of their age or other attributes that the numbers might indicate. Basically the pieces are as fine as their inherent beauty. Items marked *A-Coll.,* seemingly belonged to Tiffany personally.

It might be of interest to add that, were a book published containing several thousand different pictures of beautiful glass, a new collector could still put together an equally outstanding collection of handsome pieces not included in such a volume, since the scope of Louis C. Tiffany's work was so great.

* * * * *

Quezal

The Quezal Art Glass and Decorating Company, Brooklyn, New York, was founded by Martin Bach shortly after 1900. Bach was an employee of the Tiffany Glass Company for many years before starting his own business venture. It is not surprising, therefore, to note the great similarities in Quezal and Tiffany glass. Practically everything produced by Bach has the iridescent finish featuring contrasting colored glass threads, hooked into a "pull-up" pattern and then rolled into the outer surface of the glass while still in the plastic stage before cooling. Plates pp. 123 ff.

Production was somewhat limited as to originality of shape and pattern, but it should be remembered that each piece had to be handmade, and that without a large plant operations would naturally be limited. Commercial table ware in iridescent gold is frequently found, and in addition Martin Bach did offer a number of quite exquisite miniatures. Green, gold, and white colors predominate.

It is interesting to note that Victor Durand, some twenty years later,

Text cont. on p. 120

222. Apple bloosom Tiffany lamp, signed *Tiffany Studios, New York,* 29″, Chrysler Art Museum.

223. Dragon-fly Tiffany lamp, signed *Tiffany Studios, New York,* 29″, Chrysler Art Museum.

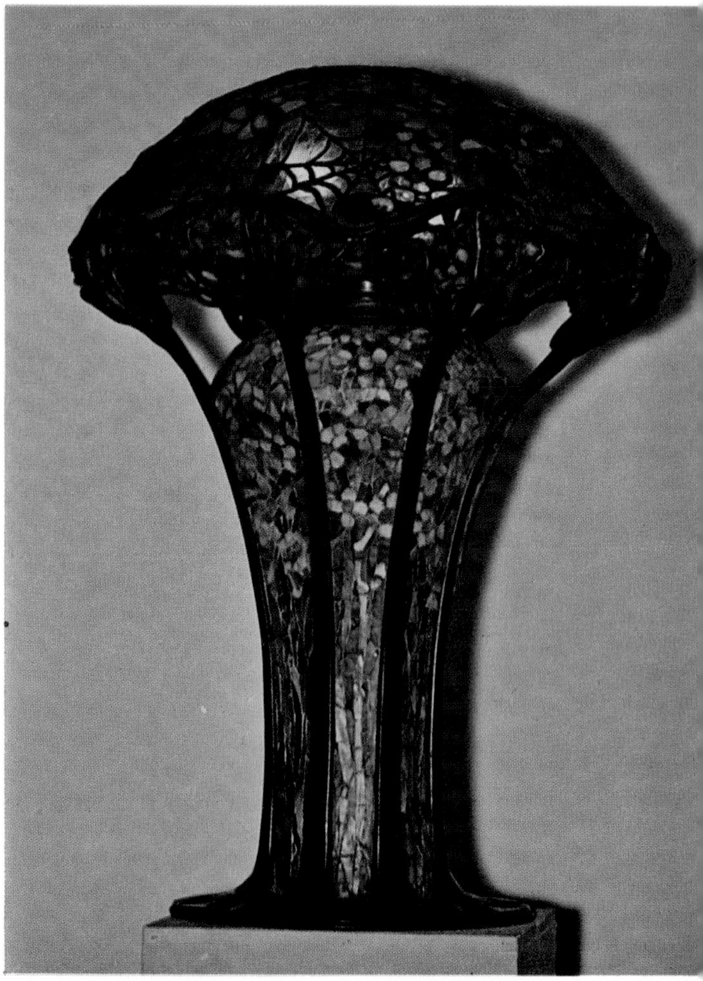

224. Spider web, apple blossom Tiffany lamp with mosaic base, signed *Tiffany Studios, New York,* 27 1/2″, Chrysler Art Museum.

Text on p. 117

225. Portrait Tiffany lamp with turtle-back design, signed *Tiffany Studios, New York,* 13″, collection of Mr. and Mrs. Barry H. Gerstein.

226. Tiffany mushroom night light, signed *Tiffany Studios, New York,* 11 1/2″, Chrysler Art Museum.

Text on p. 117

looking for qualified artist workmen to produce fine art glass, employed Martin Bach Jr., who carried on in his father's tradition.

* * * * *

Kew Blas

Plates pp. 126–27

Kew Blas art glass was a product of the Union Glass Company, Somerville, Massachusetts. This well known company, which operated almost seventy-five years, until 1924, did very beautiful work in the small lamp shade field. Their iridescent glass was limited in colors, primarily to greens, tans, browns, creamy white, and snow white colors. This does not mean that other colors were not used, but rather that these shades predominated.

One of the marks of Kew Blas ware is the seemingly exacting manner in which the patterns of colored glass in contrasting glass backgrounds were handled. Sharpness of pattern and brilliance of color are quite noticeable. There is also an absence of splotchiness, which is not uncommon in iridescent ware by other companies. In addition to their beautiful whites, the contrasting grass green color is of consistently high standard.

While the Union Glass Company had a relatively small art glass output, their ware was of extremely fine concept in color and shape. William S. Blake, Superintendent of the factory during the height of their art glass production, conceived the trade name of their ware, Kew Blas, by an interesting shifting of the letters of his name.

* * * * *

Durand

Plates pp. 128ff.

Victor Durand, a descendant of the French Baccarat family, operated a commercial glass house in Vineland, New Jersey for several decades. In the early 1920's he decided to produce a limited amount of colored art wares. Employed by him were men of considerable experience, including Emil Larsen and Martin Bach Jr., whose father operated the Quezal Art Glass and Decorating Company. Both of these men were recognized and highly experienced in their field of hand blown art glass.

A small number of pieces were signed with *Durand* written in script, usually inside of a large *V*. Occasionally there were factory numbers.

Most of Durand art glass vases were constructed of multi-layered glass with various colored glass designs rolled into and made a part of the exterior surface. Intense and brilliant color achievement is prominent in the art of Durand, who had a penchant for using eye-catching designs on a minimum number of basic shapes.

Thinly drawn glass threading applied around the main body of the ware but not rolled into the outer surface is typically Durand (Plate 240), however, this threading is quite brittle and perishable. Reds, blues, greens, and golds all hooked in combination with silver stripings are other examples of the striking Durand creations. In flatware as well as stemware the drawn white feather design on red, blue, gold, and green transparent backgrounds (Plates 249, 252 and 254) is one of Durand's finest presentations. These pieces were rarely marked, but the very nature of the work identifies itself.

The intaglio and cameo pieces shown in Plates 244 and 248, respectively, which are of great rarity, illustrate the considerable scope and imagination of Victor Durand.

* * * * *

Nash

Plates p. 134

Glass made by Arthur J. Nash and his sons in Corona, N.Y., was, for the most part, relatively unprepossessing. This is strange in view of the fact that while Tiffany became the outstanding name in American art glass achievements, Arthur J. Nash was in fact the Tiffany inside man and much of the striking and handsome work of Tiffany is attributed to his efforts.

Prior to 1900 Nash was associated with the famous Webb cameo group in England, certainly indicative of his recognized ability. After 1919 small quantities of ware appeared with the Nash signature in crude block lettering, frequently with style numbers.

The sherbet in crinkly iridescent gold, shown in Plate 255, is hardly distinguishable from its counterpart in Tiffany. This is not the case in Plate 256 where we have a pulled-up type pattern, one of the few designs recognized as a Nash creation. It was produced in many shapes, including flatware with the pattern emanating from the center, as in a cartwheel. Muted greens and browns in transparent glass predominate, as well as iridescent colored finishes in single- and double-layered glass. There is less excitement and originality of form in the glass designed by Nash, but the work is of a high quality. Both Leslie and Douglas Nash, sons of Arthur, were involved in the production and sale of this fine ware.

* * * * *

Kimball

Plates p. 135

The Kimball Glass Company, Vineland, New Jersey, produced a cluthra-type glass, quite similar to the Steuben cluthra, but without the pronounced "fried egg" bubble typical of the Steuben ware.

Shapes manufactured by Col. Ewan Kimball from 1925 through the early 1930's were of a rather plain nature and heavy construction, and had a glossy finish. Colors are quite vivid, and for the most part are somewhat less than uniform in intensity, creating a cloudy and somewhat variegated effect in the glass. This one type of art glass seems to have predominated in Kimball's work in this field.

* * * * *

Steuben

Plates pp. 136 ff.

Text cont. on p. 140

Steuben glass, in the Art Glass field, covers a period from the inception of production in 1903 through the early 1930's when the manufacture of colored glass ceased. Founded in 1903 by T. G. Hawkes of

227. Tiffany candlestick, signed *Tiffany Studios, N.Y.*, 14 1/2″, collection of Lillian Nassau.

228. Wisteria Tiffany lamp, signed *Tiffany Studios, New York,* 28 1/2″, collection of J. Jonathon Joseph.

Text on p. 117

229. Quezal vase with silver inlay decoration, signed *Quezal,* 10″, collection of Frances D. Armentrout.

Text on p. 117

230. Quezal vase, signed *Quezal,* 6″, collection of Sally A. Rose.

231. Quezal vase, signed *Quezal C* 269, 11 1/4″, collection of Mr. and Mrs. Raymond Suppes.

232. Quezal vase, signed *Quezal F*-703, 4 3/4″, collection of Mr. and Mrs. Raymond Suppes.

Text on p. 117

233. Quezal vase, signed *Quezal,* 8″, Chrysler Art Museum.

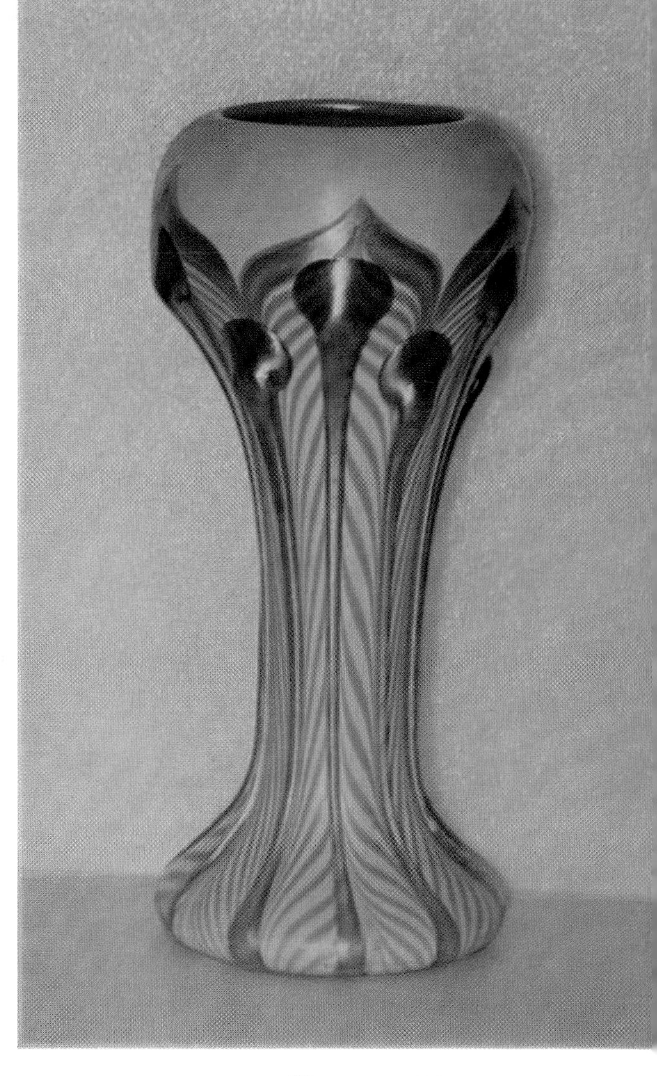

234. Quezal vase, signed *Quezal,* 11 3/4″, collection of Mr. and Mrs. Raymond Suppes.

Text on p. 117

235. Iridescent stick vase, Union Glass Co., signed *Kew Blas,* 6″, collection of Mr. and Mrs. Gerry Philpot.

236. Iridescent vase, Union Glass Co., signed *Kew Blas,* 9″, collection of Mr. and Mrs. Raymond Suppes.

237. Iridescent gold vase with butterscotch overlay trailing decoration, Union Glass Co., signed *Kew Blas,* 6″, collection of Mr. and Mrs. Raymond Suppes.

Text on p. 120

238. Iridescent Union Glass Co. vase, signed *Kew Blas,* 4 1/4″, collection of Maude B. Feld.

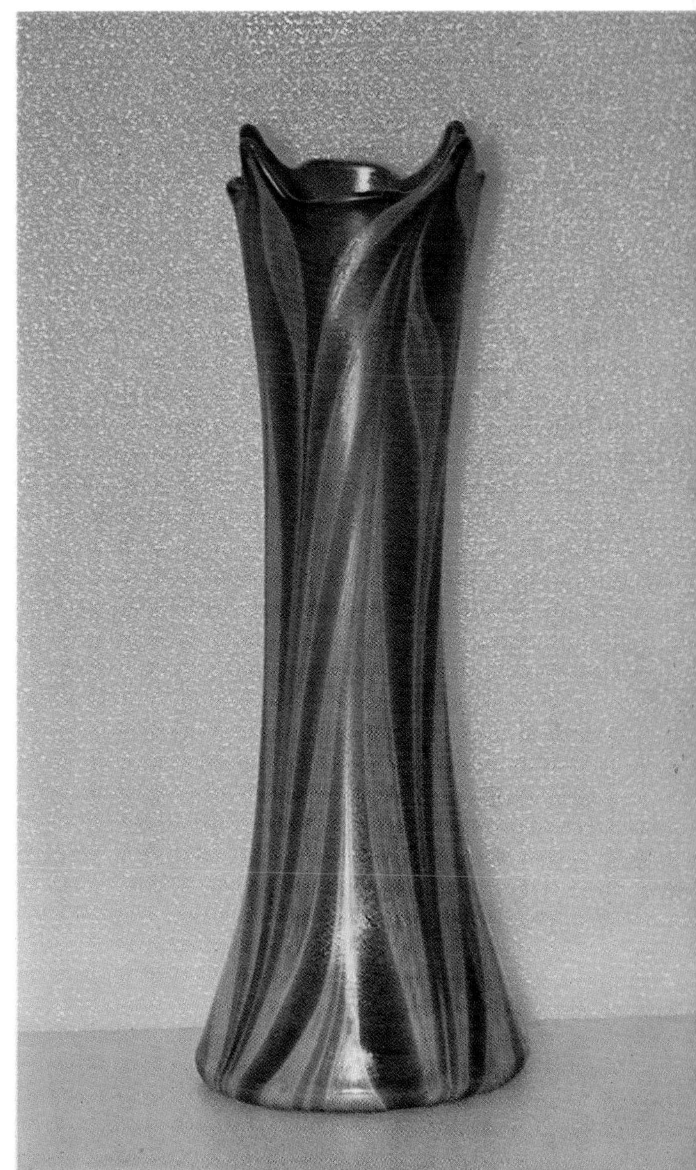

239. Irridescent Union Glass Co. vase, signed *Kew Blas,* 11 1/2″, collection of Maude B. Feld.

Text on p. 120

240. Feather pattern Durand vase with overlay threading, signed *V. Durand* 19, 9″, collection of Dr. and Mrs. Walter Donahue.

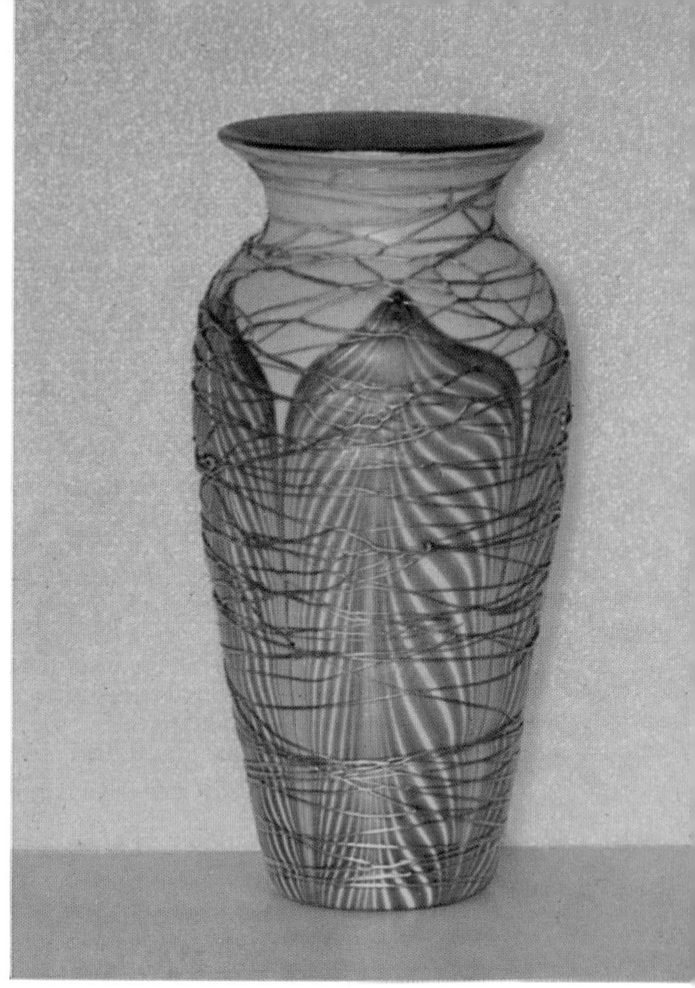

241. Covered Durand jar, signed *V. Durand 1994–8,* 11″, collection of Maude B. Feld.

242. Durand vase, signed *Durand,* 8 1/4″, Chrysler Art Museum.

Text on p. 120

243. Intaglio cut Durand vase, signed *V. Durand 20161–8,* 7 3/4″, collection of Mr. and Mrs. Raymond Suppes.

Text on p. 120

244. Intaglio cut, four-layer Durand vase, signed *V. Durand 1911–70,* 10 3/4″, collection of Frances D. Armentrout.

245. Durand vase, signed *V. Durand* 19, 10″, collection of Frances D. Armentrout.

246. Durand covered jar, 7 1/4″, Chrysler Art Museum.

Text on p. 120

247. Green triple overlay jar, signed *Durand,* 11″ collection of Frances D. Armentrout.

248. Durand cameo vase, signed *V. Durand 1995–8,* 6 1/2″, collection of Frances D. Armentrout.

Text on p. 120

249. Feather pattern Durand vase with intaglio cutting, signed *Durand,* 10″, collection of Mr. and Mrs. Raymond Suppes.

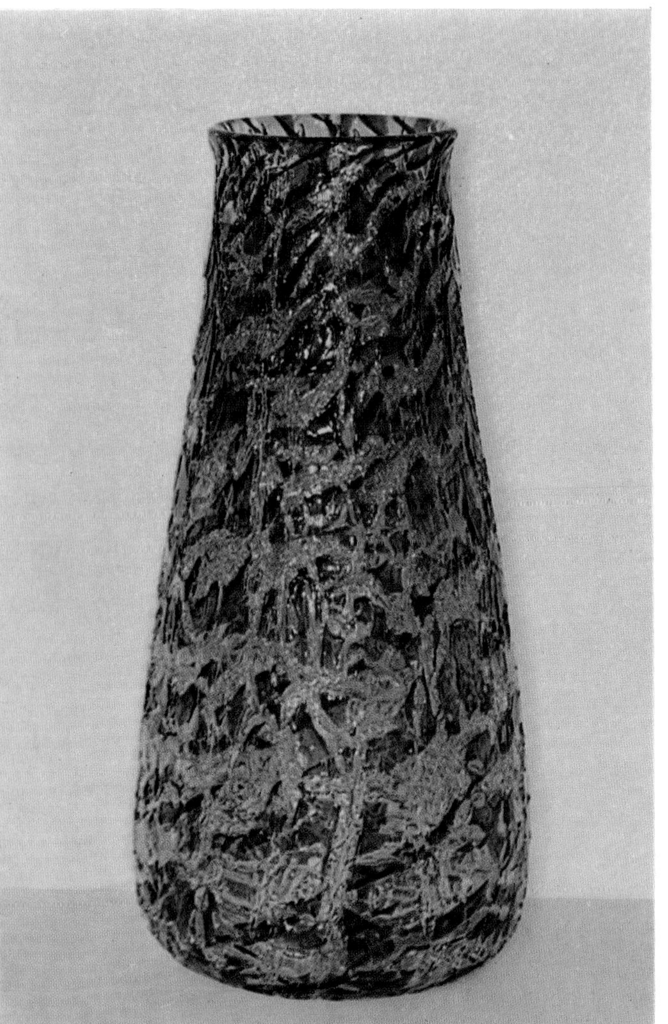

250. Blue crackle Durand vase, signed *V. Durand,* 12″, Chrysler Art Museum.

251. Red, cut overlay Durand vase, signed *V. Durand* 1968 *T 10–10,* 9 3/4″, collection of Frances D. Armentrout.

Text on p. 120

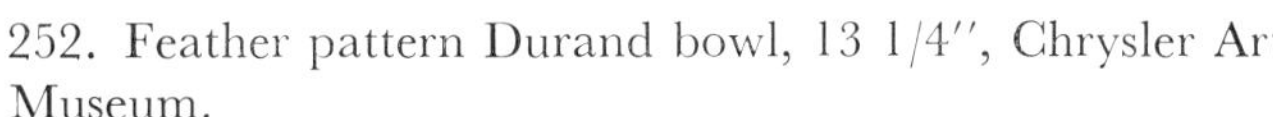

252. Feather pattern Durand bowl, 13 1/4″, Chrysler Art Museum.

253. Durand vase, signed *Durand*, 12″, collection of Frances D. Armentrout.

254. Durand sherbet, wine, and goblet, with feather pattern, 6 3/4″, collection of Frances D. Armentrout.

Text on p. 120

255. Gold iridescent Nash vase, 5 1/2, collection of Mr. and Mrs. J. Michael Pearson.

256. Gold iridescent Nash vase, signed *Nash Q D 72,* 7 1/2″, collection of Frances D. Armentrout.

Text on p. 121

257. Kimball cluthra vase, signed *K 1995–6 Dec 8*, 5″, authors' collection.

258. Kimball cluthra vase, signed *K 20170–8 Dec. 7,* 7 3/4″, Milan Historical Museum.

Text on p. 121

259. Iridescent blue decorated aurene Steuben fan vase, signed *F. Carder-Aurene, Steuben,* 8 1/2″, Rockwell Gallery.

260. Gold aurene threading on iridescent green jade Steuben vase, 10″, Rockwell Gallery.

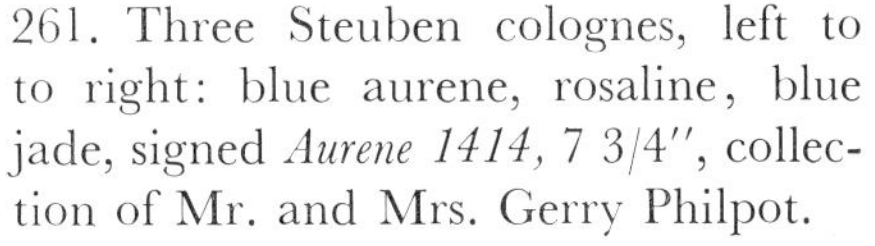

261. Three Steuben colognes, left to to right: blue aurene, rosaline, blue jade, signed *Aurene 1414,* 7 3/4″, collection of Mr. and Mrs. Gerry Philpot.

Text on p. 140

262. Iridescent red aurene Steuben bowl, signed *F. Carder,* 3″, Rockwell Gallery.

263. Iridescent red, white, and gold aurene Steuben vase, signed *F. Carder, Steuben, Aurene 298,* 9 3/4″, Rockwell Gallery.

264. Brown aurene Steuben vase, signed *F. Carder, Aurene 270,* 7 3/4″, Rockwell Gallery.

Text on p. 140

265. Iridescent aurene Steuben bowl, signed *Aurene 647,* 2 3/4″, collection of Mr. and Mrs. Raymond Suppes.

266. Iridescent green aurene Steuben bowl, signed *Aurene Q 606,* 2 3/4″, collection of Mr. and Mrs. Raymond Suppes.

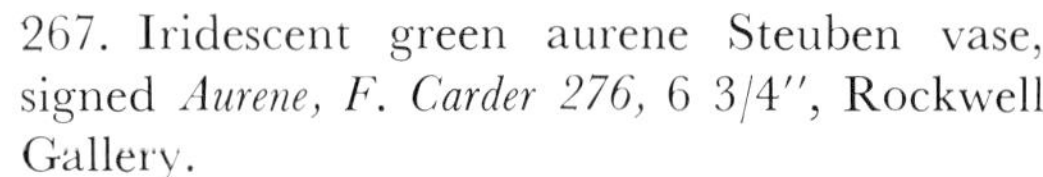

267. Iridescent green aurene Steuben vase, signed *Aurene, F. Carder 276,* 6 3/4″, Rockwell Gallery.

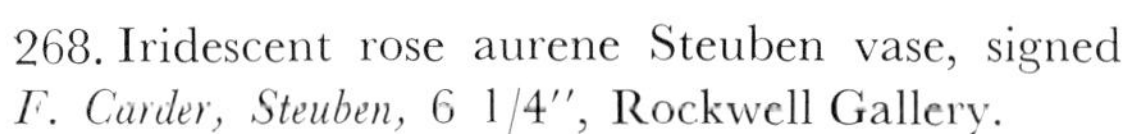

268. Iridescent rose aurene Steuben vase, signed *F. Carder, Steuben,* 6 1/4″, Rockwell Gallery.

Text on p. 140

269. Iridescent blue aurene Steuben vase, signed *Steuben aurene 7103, F. Carder*, 10″, Rockwell Gallery.

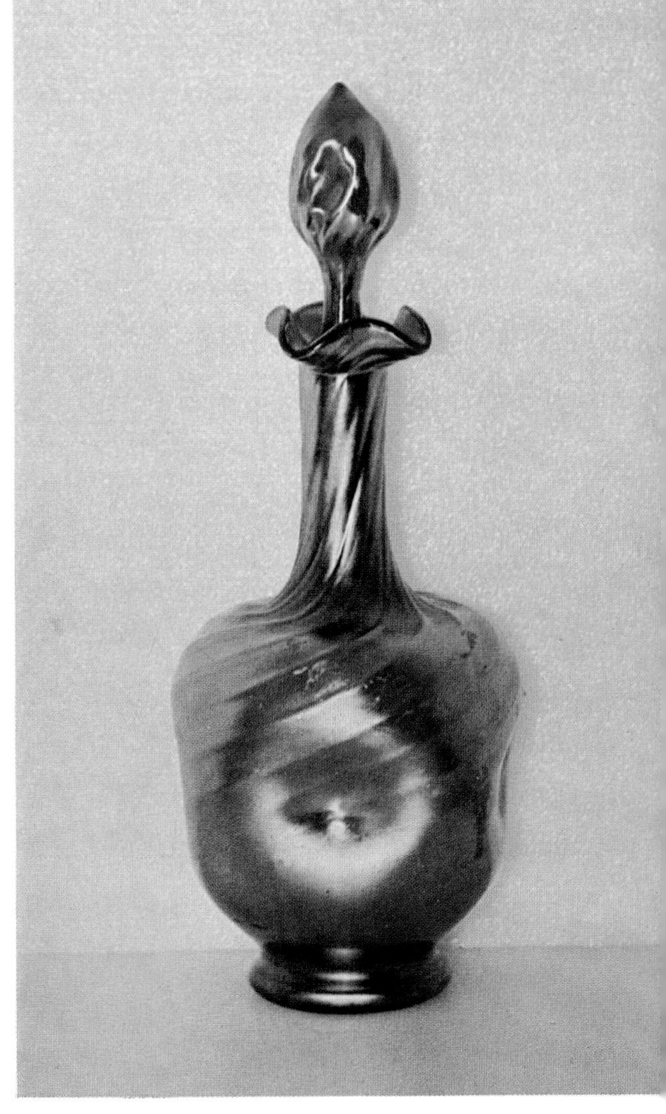

270. Iridescent green aurene Steuben decanter, signed *Aurene 799, F. Carder*, 10″, Rockwell Gallery.

Text on p. 140

Steuben (continued)

the Hawkes Glass Company and Frederick Carder, the complete operation of practically every aspect of the plant was in the hands of Carder until the sale of the plant in 1918 to the Corning Glass Works, also located in Corning, New York. Carder continued as art director until 1934, after which time his active association with Corning was limited to his own laboratory in the plant until 1953. Carder was trained in England, being the Art Director at Stevens & Williams, important glass manufacturer of fine art glass. Since he also was given a free hand in the operation of the Steuben Glass Works we can readily understand the vast field of production and experimental techniques found in the work of this company.

We find upwards of ten major categories and any number of additional minor groups of limited production. It should be realized that of necessity many of the various types overlap, as well as appear in combinations to attract the public, bearing in mind at all times that Steuben was a commercial operation depending wholly on its sales of colored glass to stay in business. This would of course account for the vast range of colors offered and the great variety of shapes, which had tremendous public appeal.

Aurene undoubtedly is the best known ware of Steuben, being a translucent glass with an iridescent finish. Gold is the most common, with blue, green, brown, and red, along with many shadings of the various colors, following in this order of rarity. Combinations of colors with stem and leaf patterns are quite usual, along with feather, or pull-up, designs which are less frequent. It would be most practical to classify Aurene as a surface finish technique, rather than a glass construction technique because you will notice several pieces of acid cutback work with Aurene finish in part. See Plate 281 as well as the millefiore Aurene shown in Plate 301.

Plates pp. 146 ff.

Jade glass is exactly what the name implies: a reflection in glass of the various colors found in that stone. Please note that green is only one of the myriad of colors found in mineral jade, contrary to the general association by most people of the word jade and the color green. Alabaster glass is basically of a translucent white, and the addition of color results in Jade glass. Combinations of the various jade colors with white alabaster trim on stems of wines and goblets are quite usual. The bodies of the pieces are in color. This should be remembered, as the one characteristic of Fry glass is that the main body of the piece is of white alabaster and the trim in color.

Occasionally Jade will be found with a satin finish (Plates 260 and 265) although this is infrequent. Jade glassware, unless marked or identified by an exclusively Steuben shape, could very easily be confused with similar ware produced by Stevens & Williams for some twenty years. The Jade glass category is, however, one of the very few types of glass identified with both Stevens & Williams, and Steuben. There are various shadings in each color, although this is primarily due to the thickness of the walls of the piece rather than to a concentration of color. Rosaline, though thought of as a separate type of glass, is, in fact, only a rose colored jade, but due to its popularity the name Rosaline has separated this color into a collectible group. Jade (colored alabaster glass) is also found as an outer layer over the white alabaster glass. When engraving or intaglio work is done on the outer colored jade we have a very beautiful example, as shown in Plate 277. In the case of acid cutback or cameo type carving, refer to the acid cutback group in which the two layers of glass are only too evident.

Cluthra glass is a partially transparent, two-layered glass, wherein chemicals fixed between the two layers create small air pockets in the center of white splotches. This effect is highly suggestive of "sunny side up, fried eggs," when the yolk of the egg is positioned, as is the air pocket in the white splotch in the glass. The air pocket, it should be pointed out, is not centered, but rather off to one side. Cluthra comes in solid colors as well as pieces shading from color to white. Contrary to popular opinion, signed pieces actually are not infrequent. Many collectors have come to this opinion, however, notwithstanding the difficulty created by the mark blending too well into the rest of the glass. When the base of the piece has been satinized or sanded off it is well nigh impossible to find the mark. The shape illustrated in Plate 278, usually with the handles, in various sizes, is probably the most common shape in the Cluthra line. Plate p. 147

Cintra glass is similar to Cluthra, with the exception that the "fried egg" effect, or bubbles, is absent. As may be noticed in the candlestick shown in Plate 279, lineal patterns are common. Cintra glass, although not in pattern decoration, may occasionally be found in acid cutback work, which lends considerable richness to what otherwise might be a somewhat flat feeling. Here again we find the mixing of glass types, i.e. Cintra and Acid Cutback. Plate p. 148

Acid Cutback, or cameo type glass, normally is made of a minimum of two layers of contrasting colored glass with the darker color most frequently being the outer layer. After the outer layer of darker glass is cut away, except for the design which has been protected from erosion by acid resisting coating, the design is left in high relief against the lighter colored under-layer of glass. This design is then worked upon by the artist, refining the decoration to a finished picture in high relief. Most of this type of work turned out at Steuben consisted of two-layer glass, although one occasionally runs across a single-layered example in camphor color. It should not be too difficult to acquire Plates pp. 150–51

Text cont. on p. 144

271. Yellow jade Steuben cologne bottle, 5 1/2", Rockwell Gallery.

272. Yellow jade with blue aurene overlay decoration, Steuben vase, 11 ", Milan Historical Museum.

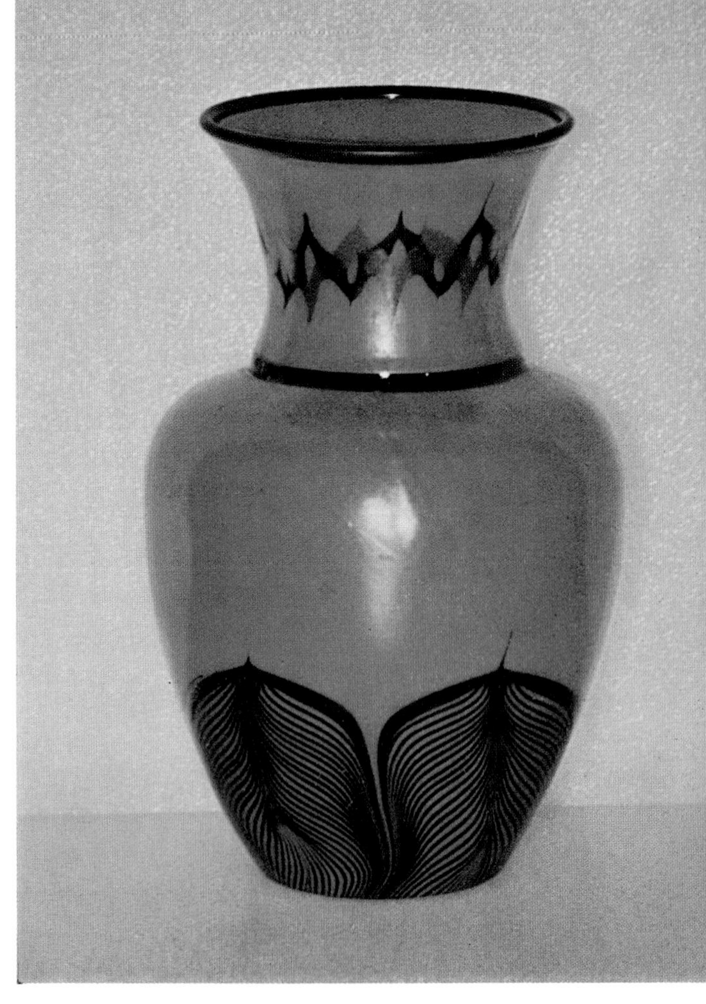

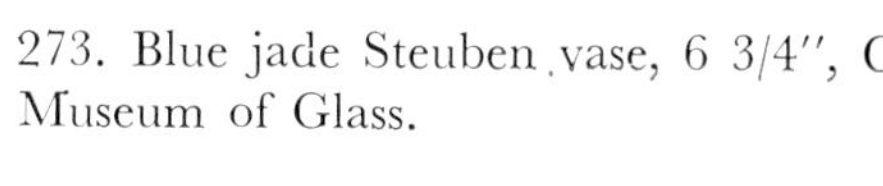

273. Blue jade Steuben vase, 6 3/4", Corning Museum of Glass.

Text on pp. 140–41

274. Blue jade Steuben tazza, signed *F. Carder, Steuben,* 8 1/2″, Rockwell Gallery.

275. Green jade Steuben prong vase, signed *Steuben,* 14 1/4″, Rockwell Gallery.

Text on pp. 140–41

an example of acid cutback work in view of the fact that close to two thousand acid cutbacks were made, many to be used as lamp bases. *Steuben (continued)* While only six patterns are shown there were reputedly several hundred different decorations used. The angular, geometric style is one of the clues to an unmarked piece of Steuben origin, and there are not too many different shapes, undoubtedly resulting from the fact that the shape was secondary to the pattern in the creation of acid cutback work.

Ivrene, a transparent, white opaque glass, might best be described as nearly pure snow white in color with a light satin finish, slightly Plate p. 149 iridescent. This work is quite rare, most of the pieces being in the art shapes rather than the commercial ware forms such as flatware, goblets, and the like.

Ivory glass, while having an appearance similar to Ivrene, is more on the creamy white side, without iridescence. It is frequently referred Plate p. 152 to as custard glass, although this would be incorrect. Whereas Ivrene is usually found without contrasting color decoration, Ivory was often used with contrasting color, and gives a very striking effect (Plate 286).

Calcite glass was used in conjunction with contrasting colored Aurenes, either on the inner or outer surface. Referring to Plate 287, a blue Plates p. 153 calcite and quite rare in this color combination, we may notice that the white calcite is on the exterior, with a lining of blue Aurene. Gold calcite is not uncommon. We have seen a single piece of non-iridescent green calcite, and no doubt other color combinations were experimented with. This ware was used in table settings, including small sauce dishes, sherbets, and nut or candy dishes. When found, the blue is of uniformly outstanding color and iridescence.

Plate p. 154 Sculptured glass covers a rather wide range of techniques, with the ultimate aim to depict figural subjects including animals, busts, and high relief heads of well known people. The simplest type of sculptured work is that done by casting directly into a mold. The mold is then opened and the piece emerges fairly complete. Of greater rarity is the Cire Perdue method wherein undercutting is necessary. A wax model of the object is made and then covered with a plaster cast. When the plaster cast is heated the wax runs out leaving a hollow cast which is then filled with ground glass in powder form. When heated, this finely-ground glass reaches a liquid state, after which it is allowed to cool and harden naturally. The plaster cast is then removed from the hardened glass model. A fine example of this is shown in Plate 289, a candlestick with the head of Electra representing light. While not depicted, there Plates p. 155 is another head carved on the other side of the stick. Diatreta, or latticework application, is beautifully shown in Plates 290 and 291. The main body of the piece is a bowl with the outer lattice work a fraction of an inch away from and surrounding the bowl and attached to the outer surface of the piece by tiny glass struts. This type undoubtedly is the rarest and most difficult type of glass construction. While there are several pieces of European Diatreta work known to exist, viewing any piece, regardless of origin or age, is a rare treat.

Verre de Soie, translated from the French to mean glass of silk, has just such a smooth iridescent finish. As seen in Plate 292, the piece would be almost transparent without the iridescence. Occasionally Plate p. 158 the palest of green color is added in the manufacture of Verre de Soie, but practically all the ware is of a soft camphor colored appearance.

Transparent glass, crystal clear, is the outstanding trade mark of the glass produced by Steuben since 1934, and for which the plant is justifiably world famous. Prior to 1934, however, this type of glass was Plates p. 159 produced in a whole range of colors and shapes. Plate 295 depicting two cologne bottles, utilitarian pieces, as well as Plate 294, in the shape of a thorny, three-branch tree formation, are fine examples of this colored crystal glass. Plate 296, showing a stoppered pitcher, demonstrates the effect of red crystal cherries used as an overlay decoration. Threaded glass (Plate 293) illustrates the striking effect of black threading being rolled almost flush into the clear, colorless body of the piece. Most frequently, however, the threading stands out in low relief on the outer surface of the pieces. Another item (Plate 297) illustrates silenium red glass with engraving consisting of leaf and grape pattern. A quantity of this silenium red, clear glass was evidently made for table settings. Plate p. 162

Bubbly glass would also fall into the clear glass category, running in a full range of colors, with tiny bubbles throughout the body of the glass.

Intarsia glass, once seen, is never forgotten, as it consists of an extremely sharp pattern of colored glass, sandwiched between an inner and outer layer of clear glass. The process used in the manufacture of Plate p. 163 this glass is similar to that of inlaying contrasting colors of wood in a table top and then covering it over with a clear, protective coating. Very few of these pieces were ever made. In view of the fact that only one workman, along with Carder, ever produced these Intarsia pieces, the claim that every piece of true Intarsia is signed, would seem to be quite likely.

Paperweight glass pieces consist of a pattern of colored glasses laid on the surface of the inner body of the glass and then covered with a coating of clear glass. A bird on a tree branch (Plate 299) is one of the Plate p. 164 seldom found examples of this type.

Moss Agate glass simulates the colors as they are found in the mineral Plate p. 165 moss agate. Shown in Plate 300, this ware is very rich in warm colors Text cont. on p. 156

276. Royal blue jade Steuben vase, signed *F. Carder, Steuben*, 12″, Rockwell Gallery.

277. Rosaline Steuben vase with intaglio cutting, signed *Fleur de Lis* mark, 12″, Rockwell Gallery.

Text on p. 141

278. Cluthra Steuben vase, signed *F. Carder-Steuben,* 10″, Rockwell Gallery.

Text on p. 141

279. Cintra Steuben candlestick, signed *F. Carder, Steuben,* 10″, Rockwell Gallery.

Text on p. 141

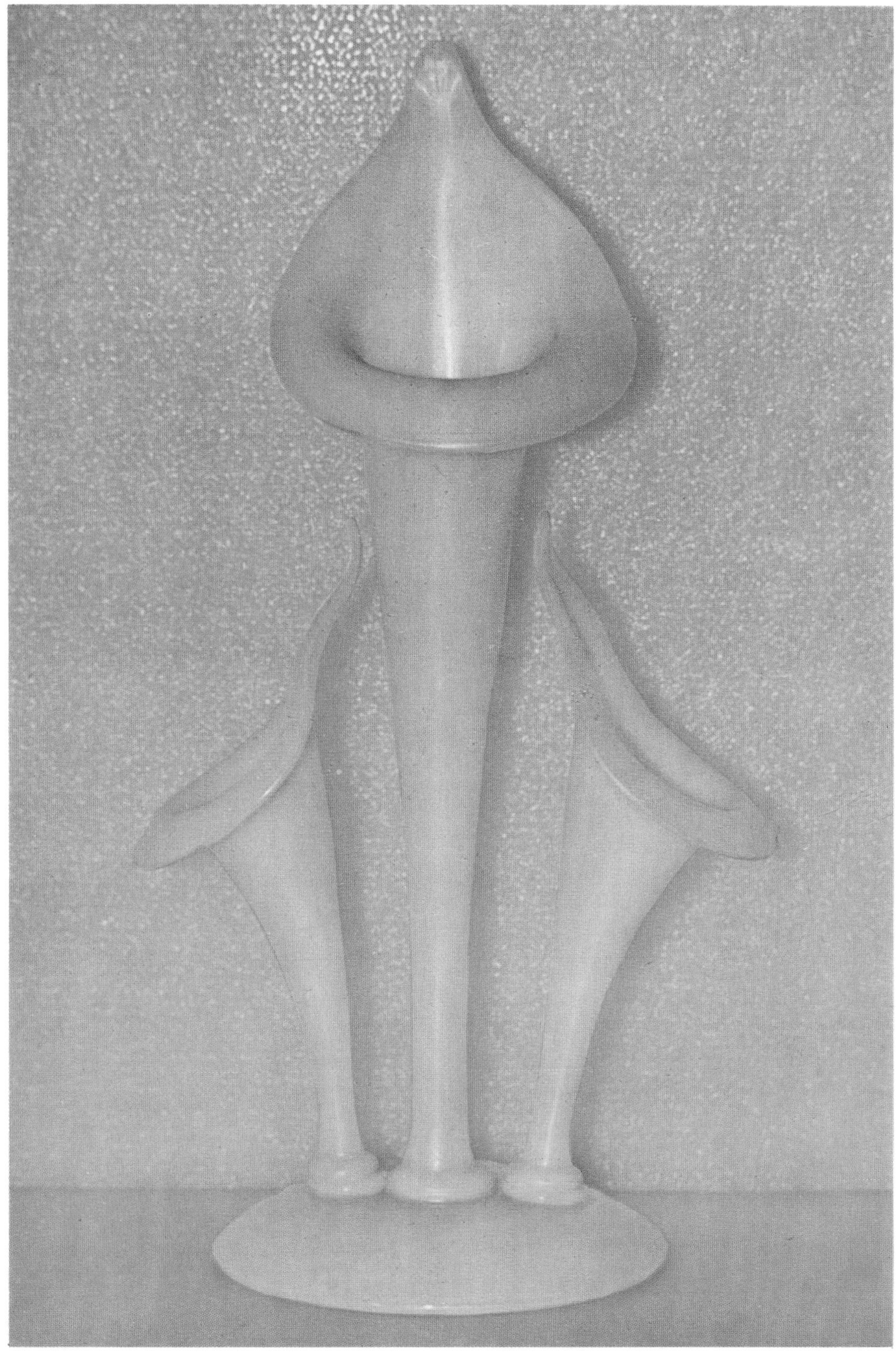

280. Steuben Ivrene lily vase, signed *Steuben,* 12 1/4″, Rockwell Gallery.

Text on p. 144

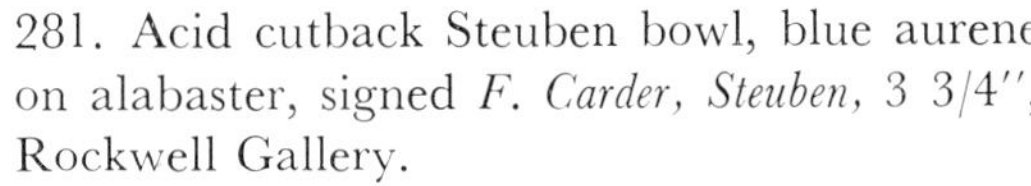

281. Acid cutback Steuben bowl, blue aurene on alabaster, signed *F. Carder, Steuben,* 3 3/4″, Rockwell Gallery.

282. Acid cutback Steuben vase, signed *Fredrk Carder,* 12″, Rockwell Gallery.

283. Acid cutback Steuben vase, 11 1/2″, Rockwell Gallery.

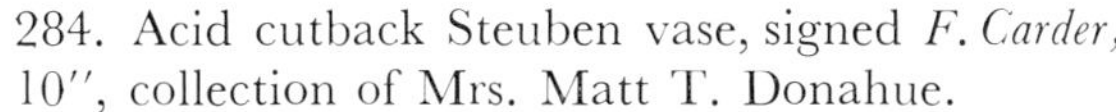

284. Acid cutback Steuben vase, signed *F. Carder,* 10″, collection of Mrs. Matt T. Donahue.

285. Acid cutback Steuben vase, signed *F. Carder-Steuben,* 14″, Rockwell Gallery.

Text on p. 141

286. Ivory Steuben vase, signed *Fredrk Carder, Steuben,* 9 3/4″, Rockwell Gallery.

Text on p. 144

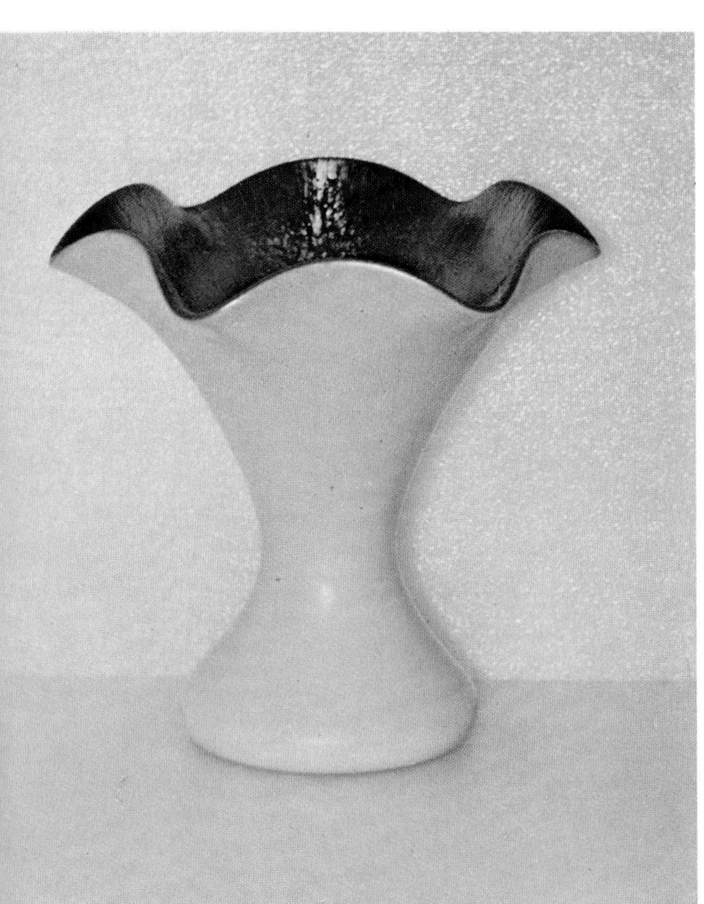

287. Blue calcite Steuben vase, 6″, collection of Mrs. Matt T. Donahue.

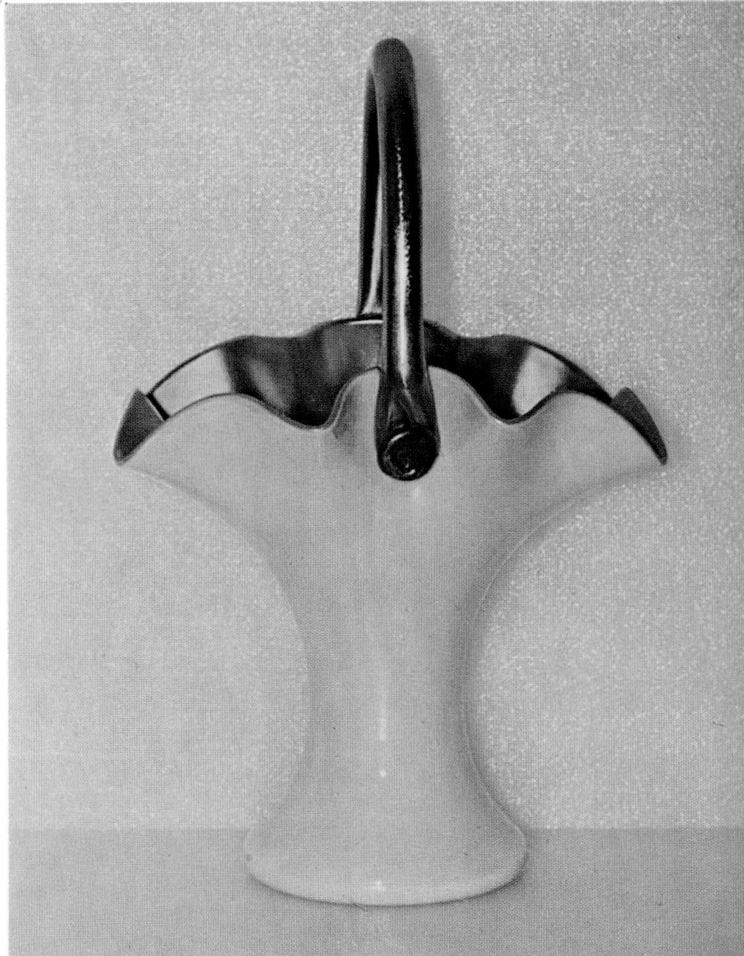

288. Gold calcite Steuben basket, signed *F. Carder, Aurene,* 9 1/4″, Rockwell Gallery.

Text on p. 144

289. Cire Perdue Steuben candlestick, signed *F. Carder,* 9″, collection of Mrs. Matt T. Donahue.

Text on p. 144

290. Diatreta Steuben vase, signed *F. Carder,* 6″, Corning Museum of Glass.

291. Diatreta Steuben vase, signed *F. Carder,* 8″, Corning Museum of Glass.

Text on pp. 144–45

Steuben (continued)

running into the browns, blues, and reds. Colored glass powders trapped internally in the glass in random patterns identify Moss Agate by Steuben. English, as well as continental sources turned out glass of the same name, but having once seen Steuben Moss Agate, there can be no confusion due to the radical difference in colors.

Plate p. 166

Millefiore glass, as pictured in Plate 305, consists of small millefiore canes of glass, sliced very thin and imbedded in the surface of the piece. These canes are most frequently found set in an Aurene, iridescent finish glass, usually in the art forms, rarely in commercial work.

Plates p. 167

Rouge Flambe glass is one of the most strikingly explosive red shades achieved in glass. In view of the exact control needed for the mix, as well as the proper heat of the fire, very little variation may occur before a piece falls short of its natural brilliance. Referring to Plate 303 we see blue Aurene inlaid decoration with an overall beautiful iridescence, as well as in the plain Rouge Flambe plate (Plate 302). These pieces must be recognized, as they were rarely signed, but using Steuben shapes as reference along with the outstanding red color, it is highly unlikely that one will overlook such a piece.

Plates p. 168

Unique works of which only a few individual examples exist, either due to lack of demand, expense of production, and actual lack of competent artist-workmen to achieve the unusually high standards demanded by Carder, include the Mica Fleck vase also known as Floventia (Plate 307), the paperweight cologne (Plate 304), the all over millefiore bowl which was one of the earliest achievements by Carder himself (Plate 305), and the Tyrian piece shown in Plate 306. The few pieces of Tyrian work that we have seen all bear the name "Tyrian" underfoot.

With Frederick Carder in overall charge of Steuben for so many years, and with the never ending challenge to develop and present the new and unusual, it is not surprising that the Steuben policy was to seldom continue production of a piece for more than a year. Stray pieces—surprises themselves in shape and color—are constantly appearing. Their origin is beyond question, for Steuben marks on the pieces indicate their origin. A fleur-de-lis with the name "Steuben" incorporated within is probably the most common, along with the plain block letter name. On acid cutback work the occasional identification is on the lower outside of the piece, in the same fleur-de-lis, but in cameo. Other marks are likely to occur including a single "S", but this was used for only a very short time inasmuch as it was also used by another company, Sinclair. The best identification of course is the shape. In the latter years of his life Frederick Carder would authenticate unsigned pieces with his "F. Carder," and either the Aurene or Steuben signature. There should be no questioning of his ability to identify work due to his advanced age, as we personally had occasion to visit with him only a few months before his passing, and there was at no time any question as to his mental accuracy.

The Steuben Glass Works had an organization for distribution in the United States and also overseas, and thus the collector is unlimited in his search for their fine, colored art glass.

* * * * *

English Cameo

Plates pp. 169ff.

Other than applied decoration, there are two methods of executing designs on glass: intaglio and cameo. Intaglio work is the process of cutting the design into the outer surface, and is also termed engraving, or etching.

Cameo, or raised design decoration, normally requires two or more layers of glass laminated together by heat. These cameo designs on the outer layer of colored glass are left in relief by removing the glass surrounding the design. This surplus outer layer is removed with acid as well as by chiselling, grinding tools, and wheels. The desired decoration on the outer layer is protected from destruction by the corrosive acid by coating the cameo design with an acid resisting material. After the acid consumes the glass surrounding the protected area the contrasting colored underlayer is revealed. The protective, acid resistant material is then removed from the outer layer and we now have the cameo work in a crude state.

Small cutting and grinding tools are then employed to finely shape and thin out the outerlayer design, or cameo decoration. By shaving down this cameo to an extreme thinness the secondary layer of contrasting colored glass begins to show through, creating a new three dimension perspective of depth in the cameo. This is accomplished by the development of shadows.

When more than two layers of glass are used, we have what is termed a three-, four-, or even five-colored cameo piece. See Plate 326.

It is also possible to place small and independent colored globs of glass at various places on the outer layer and then work these individual colored chunks into the desired shape and decoration. Refer to Plate 331.

To achieve fine results, several highly skilled artists are required, among them being a glassblower, pattern designer, acid etcher or grinder, and polisher. Of course the most important individual is a man to head the team, tolerating and accepting nothing less than the best, and possessing the concept of just what is perfection.

John Northwood, born in 1836, worked until about 1860 in the glass firm of W.H.B. and J. Richardson, learning, experimenting, and developing practical methods of acid etching and cutting. This great artist started his own company in 1860, first with other men, but eventually with only his brother Joseph, continuing for some twenty years

Text cont. on p. 160

292. Verre de Soie Steuben decanter, signed *F. Carder, Steuben,* 8″, Rockwell Gallery.

Text on p. 145

293. Black threaded Steuben covered jar, signed *F. Carder, Steuben,* 8 1/2″, Rockwell Gallery.

294. Crystal cerise Steuben thorn vase, signed *F. Carder, Steuben,* 5 3/4″, Rockwell Gallery.

Text on p. 145

295. Steuben cologne bottles, 12 1/2″, collection of Mr. and Mrs. Raymond Suppes.

296. Steuben decanter with overlay cherries, signed *F. Carder, Steuben,* 11″, Rockwell Gallery.

English Cameo (continued)

to create work for other companies as well as his own. During this period many of the outstanding workmen in the trade learned from and were associated with John Northwood in the carving of cameo glass. During the early part of the 1880's John Northwood, senior, became director and technical head of Stevens & Williams, the well known English glass company. It was thus, until the end of his life in 1902, John Northwood who guided the policies and became the leader of the Northwood team at Stevens & Williams. Art glass cut, enameled, and in fact, in every style and type, seemingly was produced by this company under the direction of John Northwood.

Plates pp. 169–70

Paralleling the development, creation, and marketing of this fine colored as well as clear glassware, were many other companies, the most important and outstanding in the field being Thomas Webb & Sons, who have continued in operation to this day.

Plates pp. 171 ff.

George Woodall, 1850–1925, and his brother Thomas Woodall, 1849–1926, learned the glass trade as apprentices under the guidance of John Northwood, Sr. The Woodall brothers, not only glass men but also great artists in painting and design, left Northwood in 1874, and for most of their active lives thereafter were employed by Thomas Webb & Sons. As a matter of fact even after their retirement from daily activity with Webb, about 1911, they continued their association with that company, producing fine work in a limited manner. The Woodall brothers were not always compatible with each other, as is frequently true of great individual and independent thinking artists. George Woodall is the better known of the two.

Plates pp. 178–79

The "Woodall team," which included other famous men besides the brothers themselves, accounted for the greatest number of fine cameo glass pieces in the English field. Records were kept of many of the great works produced by Webb, and without any question, the most sought after, and deservedly so, in the cameo glass world today are pieces signed by George or George and Thomas Woodall. It should not be overlooked that it was not solely the Woodalls themselves who accounted for the quality of work produced, but in fact the unyielding requirements of the various leaders of Thomas Webb & Sons who did not compromise but demanded only the best.

Not all the work produced by Webb, or Stevens & Williams, was signed. Identification of the quality work produced by these two leaders in the English cameo field is, however, not too difficult. Many shapes and designs were typical of one or the other company. Butterflies appearing in the design do not of themselves designate origin.

Here again in the cameo field when we had a choice of signed or unsigned pieces we chose the signed ones. Various marks of Webb were used, including the words "Gem Cameo," appearing on many of their more outstanding pieces. Much of the simulated ivory cameo work was unsigned, including many of the finer quality pieces. Refer to Plate 391.

A great number of outstanding men in the English cameo field have not been mentioned. We have stressed the names of Northwood, Woodall, Stevens & Williams, and Webb. Other great men included Jules Barbe, H.J. Boam, Thomas Bott, Frederick Carder, Tom Farmer, J.T. Fereday, Wm. Fritsche, Edwin Grice, T. Guest, James Hill, Joshua Hodgetts, F.E. Kny, Harry Kny, Ludwig Kny, F. Kretschman, Alphonse Lechevrel, Joseph Locke, J. Millward, Joseph Muckley, John Northwood, 2nd, Joseph Northwood, William Northwood, J.M. O'Fallon, W. Orchard, Philip Pargeter, Daniel Pearce, Lionel Pearce, Apsley Pellatt, Benjamin Richardson, H.G. Richardson, Sir Benjamin Stone, and the three sons of Thomas Webb: Thomas Wilkes, Charles, and Walter Wilkes.

A number of these men came to the United States, two of whom became particularly well known due to their outstanding creations. Frederick Carder, co-founder with T.G. Hawkes of the Steuben Glass Company, Corning, New York, in 1903, headed that company until 1918, when it was acquired by The Corning Glass Works. Carder continued his association with the satelite Steuben Glass Works until his death at the age of one hundred years, in 1963.

Joseph Locke, inventor and designer for the New England Glass Company and the Libbey Glass Co., in Cambridge, Massachusetts, and Toledo, Ohio, respectively, is undoubtedly better known for his achievements in the American glass field.

Unquestioned is the importance of each one of this group of recognized men in establishing the overall strength and importance of the cameo field, which is as strong today as when this ware was originally produced. Pieces of English Cameo Glass, with the finest of carving and minute detail, stand alone in the history of glassmaking as masterpieces of an era in the manufacture of glass that has never been surpassed.

* * * * *

Alexandrite

Plates p. 182

Appearing about 1900, and primarily of English origin, Alexandrite is a single-layered glass of three blended colors. Starting with an amber colored glass, reheating is done to certain portions of a piece, creating a fuchsia shade. Limited parts of the fuchsia colored section are again reheated, with a blue color resulting. In the pieces of this three-colored ware the center is usually amber, shading to fuchsia and then to blue on the outer rim. Alexandrite glass is found in plain as well as patterned surfaces.

While this ware, of only limited production, is thought to have come only from two firms, Thomas Webb & Sons and Stevens & Williams,

Text cont. on p. 180

297. Silenium red, engraved Steuben goblet, signed *F. Carder, Steuben,* 5 3/4″, Rockwell Gallery.

Text on p. 145

298. Intarsia Steuben vase, signed with a *Fleur de Lis* mark and *Fredrk Carder*, 6″, collection of Mr. and Mrs. Gerry Philpot.

Text on p. 145

299. Cintra paperweight Steuben vase, bluebird on a branch, 8 1/4″, Rockwell Gallery.

Text on p. 145

300. Moss Agate Steuben vase, signed *F. Carder,* 11 3/4″, Rockwell Gallery.

Text on pp. 145, 156

301. Millefiore, iridescent gold aurene Steuben vase, signed *Aurene 599,* 5 1/2", Rockwell Gallery.

Text on p. 156

302. Rouge flambe Steuben plate, signed *F. Carder,* 8 1/2″, Rockwell Gallery.

303. Decorated rouge flambe vase, signed *Fredrk Carder, Aurene,* 4 1/2″, Rockwell Gallery.

Text on p. 156

304. Steuben paperweight cologne bottle, signed *F. Carder 1918,* 8 1/2″, Rockwell Gallery.

305. Millefiore Steuben plate, signed *F. Carder, Steuben,* 11″, Rockwell Gallery.

306. Tyrian Steuben vase, signed *F. Carder,* 101/4″, Rockwell Gallery.

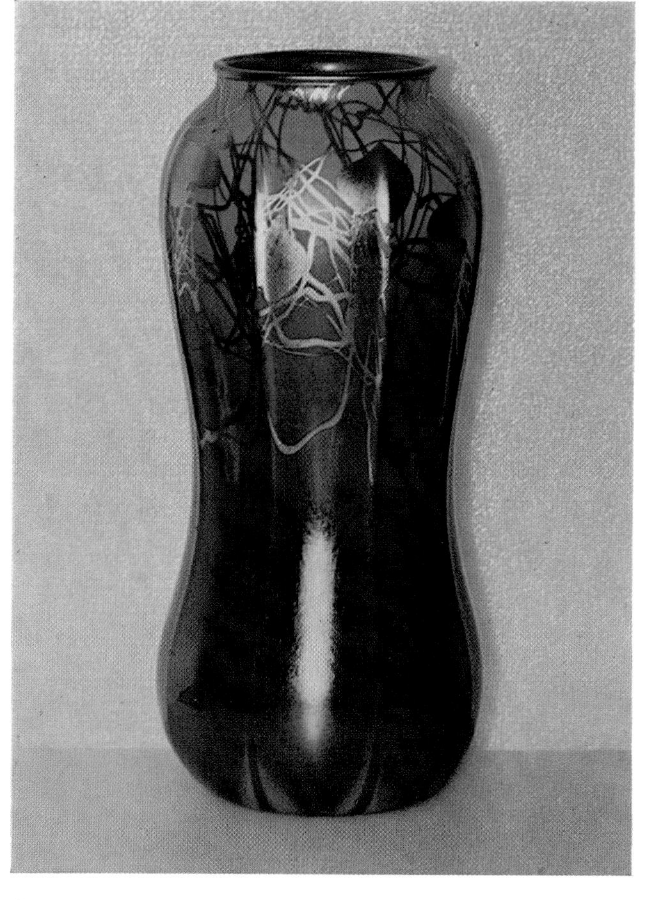

307. Mica flecked, satin finish Steuben vase, signed *F. Carder, Steuben,* 7″, Rockwell Gallery.

Text on p. 156

308. Cameo vase, signed *J. Millward 12, Stevens and Williams,* 11 3/4″, collection of Robert Jacobs.

309. Cameo vase, signed *Stevens and Williams Art Glass Stourbridge,* 8″, collection of Sally A. Rose.

Text on p. 160

310. Cameo vase, signed *Stevens and Williams, Art Glass Stourbridge,* 4 3/4″, collection of Mr. and Mrs. Gerry Philpot.

311. Dolce-Relievo cameo Stevens and Williams vase, 4″, Rockwell Gallery.

312. Cameo vase, signed *Stevens and Williams,* 9″, collection of Robert Jacobs.

313. Cameo vase, signed *Stevens and Williams, Art Glass, Stourbridge,* 6 3/4″, collection of Arthur Gabler.

Text on p. 160

314. Three-color vase, signed *Thomas Webb and Sons,* 9 1/2″, collection of Maude B. Feld.

315. Mother of Pearl vase, Thomas Webb and Sons, 7 3/4″, Milan Historical Museum.

Text on p. 160

316. Three-color cameo vase, signed *Thomas Webb and Sons,* 9″, collection of of Arthur Gabler.

317. Simulated Ivory with enamelling cameo vase, signed *Thomas Webb and Sons,* 12 1/2″, authors' collection.

318. Three-color cameo vase, signed *Thomas Webb and Sons,* 9″, authors' collection.

Text on p. 160

319. Three-color cameo vase, signed *Thomas Webb and Sons,* 5 1/2″, collection of Sally A. Rose.

320. Cameo vase, signed *Thomas Webb and Sons,* 10″, collection of Sally A. Rose.

321. Three-layer cameo vase, signed *Thomas Webb and Sons,* 6 3/4″, collection of Maude B. Feld.

Text on p. 160

322. Pair of ivory cameo vases, signed *Webb,* 5 1/4″, collection of Mr. and Mrs. Raymond Suppes.

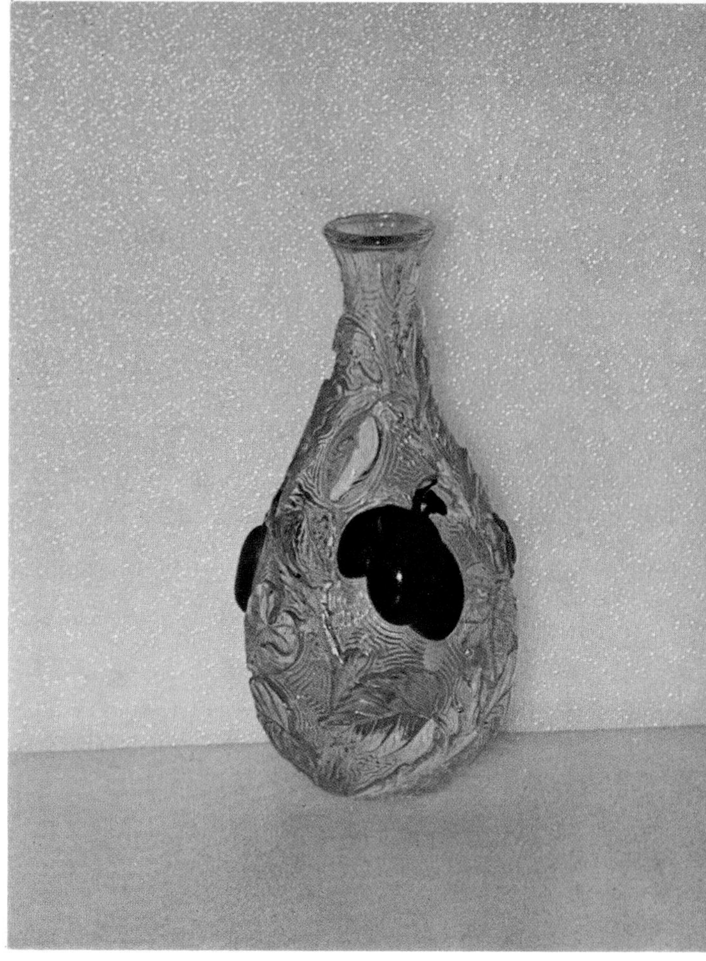

323. Cameo vase, signed *Thomas Webb and Sons,* 6″, collection of Lillian Nassau.

324. Cameo finger bowl and plate, both pieces signed *Thomas Webb and Sons, Cameo, Patent,* 5 3/4″, collection of Dr. and Mrs. M. M. Nuckolls.

Text on p. 160

325. Webb cameo gourd-shaped vase, 11 1/2″, authors' collection.

326. Webb cameo, five-color vase, 18 1/4″, collection of Sally A. Rose.

Text on p. 160

327. Webb cameo three-color inkwell, 6″, collection of Sally A. Rose.

328. Webb cameo three-color decanter, 9 1/2″, authors' collection.

329. Webb cameo bowl with two dragons, 6 1/4″, private collection.

330. Webb cameo bowl, 4 1/2″, collection of Maude B. Feld.

Text on p. 160

331. Webb cameo vase, attributed to Daniel and Lionel Pearce, 5 1/2″, collection of Robert Jacobs.

332. Webb cameo ivory stick vase, 8 3/4″, collection of Mr. and Mrs. Raymond suppes.

333. Webb cameo simulated ivory vase with enamelling, 11 1/2″, authors' collection.

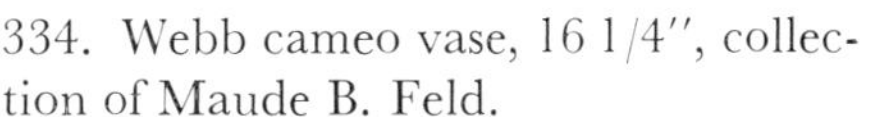

334. Webb cameo vase, 16 1/4″, collection of Maude B. Feld.

Text on p. 160

335. Webb cameo vase, signed *Diana G. W. 26, George Woodall,* 7″, collection of Dr. and Mrs. Alick Osofsky.

336. Cameo vase, signed *Thomas Webb and Sons, Gem Cameo, G.Woodall,* 7 1/2″, collection of Dr. and Mrs. Walter Donahue.

337. Webb cameo plaque, signed *Geo Woodall,* 7 3/4″, collection of Robert Jacobs.

Text on p. 160

338. Cameo vase, signed *Geo Woodall, Thomas Webb and Sons,* 13″, collection of Sally A. Rose.

Text on p. 160

both of England, there is certainly no reason to believe that any fine American company could not have experimented and produced similar colored ware. The quality of Alexandrite is usually determined by the deep richness and blending of the colors.

* * * * *

Silveria

Plates p. 183

Produced by Stevens & Williams, England, Silveria glass is frequently found with the large "S" and "W" initials joined together in script. The word "England" may sometimes appear. A small fleur-de-lis with the S and W initials might also be used.

This two-layered glass, made about 1900, normally has practically a solid sheet of silver foil trapped between the inner and outer layers of crystal. In addition, vertical drippings of colored glass, usually transparent green, wander over the piece in no regular pattern or design.

The original silver lustre is retained by the exclusion of air from the silver foil; however, when a surface crazing of the outside layer occurs and air reaches the inner foil, oxidation takes place and results in discoloration. These rare and unusual pieces of glass have a ground pontil. They make an important addition to any fine collection.

* * * * *

Silvered

Plate p. 187

Silvered Glass is not too familiar a name to the American collector. When silvered colored ware is pointed out, he recognizes it as Mercury glass, whether it is of the early 20th century or the fine mid-19th-century era. Quite prevalent is the fifty-year-old so-called Mercury, of hollow construction and extremely light in weight. Most of this is greatly discolored from oxidation, which causes black spots to appear. Corks and other perishable plugs were used for sealing the pieces in the bottom to prevent moisture and air from reaching the inside of the pieces and thereby corroding the silver mercury application on the back of the glass.

Nothing finer in this type of ware was ever produced than that in the 1850's by Varnish & Company, England. In contrast to the light weight ware mentioned above, the silvered glass produced by Varnish and others of that period was comprised of two layers of glass, quite heavy in weight. The silver reflection shows no discoloration as these articles were permanently sealed. In addition to a clear outer layer of glass, green, blue, and red colored transparent outer casings were also used. Referring to Plate 348 we notice the attractive results that were achieved by carving of the outer layer of colored glass, revealing the silver reflecting inner layer. While there were numerous manufacturers of this type in other parts of Europe as well as in England, Varnish & Company was recognized as the peer. Instead of normal incising being used to mark the factory name on the piece, Varnish, Hale Thomson, and others, made use of a stamped metallic disc one-half inch in diameter, imbedded underfoot.

* * * * *

In an effort to identify for the reader pieces likely to be found in any Shop, but relatively unknown, we have grouped the following.

Miscellaneous English

Plate 350 shows Richardson's Vitrified ware, an 1850 product of one of the outstanding firms of the day. Detailed enameling is exquisite, and the fine quality of the decoration belies the actual age of the ware.

Plates pp. 186ff.

Plates 346 and 345 show examples of Thomas Webb & Sons' Iridescent glass and Bronze glass respectively. We have only seen one signed piece, but Webb enjoyed considerable success with this work in the 1880 period. Due to the similarity in shapes and colors to the large production of American iridescent glass, pieces more often than not are attributed to such factories as Tiffany, Steuben, Durand, and the like. It should be remembered, however, that these factories produced their work with the iridescence on the exterior of the outer surface, while the Webb items, illustrated, have a smooth and glossy outer surface. It is practically mirror-like in appearance. In addition to Webb, many European as well as American companies produced work of some likeness. There is, however, a particular feel to so-called "Webb shapes."

Plate 347 shows intaglio cut, or engraved work, wherein finely detailed carving was accomplished on the outer pink layer. Decoration on the piece shown consists of many fish and floral motifs repeated in the three major bandings. While there might be some immediate confusion with Mt. Washington Glass Company work due to the outer pink layer, it will be noticed that the inner lining tends to a cream-tinged white, while Mt. Washington comes closer to a flat snow white. In addition to this feature the highly intricate intaglio work of Webb was not done by the Mt. Washington factory.

Plate 352, showing a threaded glass bowl, can at best only be attributed to English origin. More to the point in determining origin, would be the foot, typical of English work. Machines were invented and put to almost immediate use by most of the major glass companies in this country and abroad. These machines took the thin glass threads and mechanically threaded them around the outer surface. Hooks were then used to achieve loop and other patterns. Plates 353 and 354 show examples of similar methods of applications in what is known as the pull-up pattern. The piece in Plate 353 is attributed to Stevens and Williams due to the characteristic of a clear outer casing, while that in Plate 354 lacks this feature and has a satin finish, and is attributed to John Northwood. It should be remembered that after some twenty years in business with his brother Joseph, commencing in 1860, John

Text cont. on p. 184

339. Alexandrite wine glass, 4 1/2″, Milan Historical Musum.

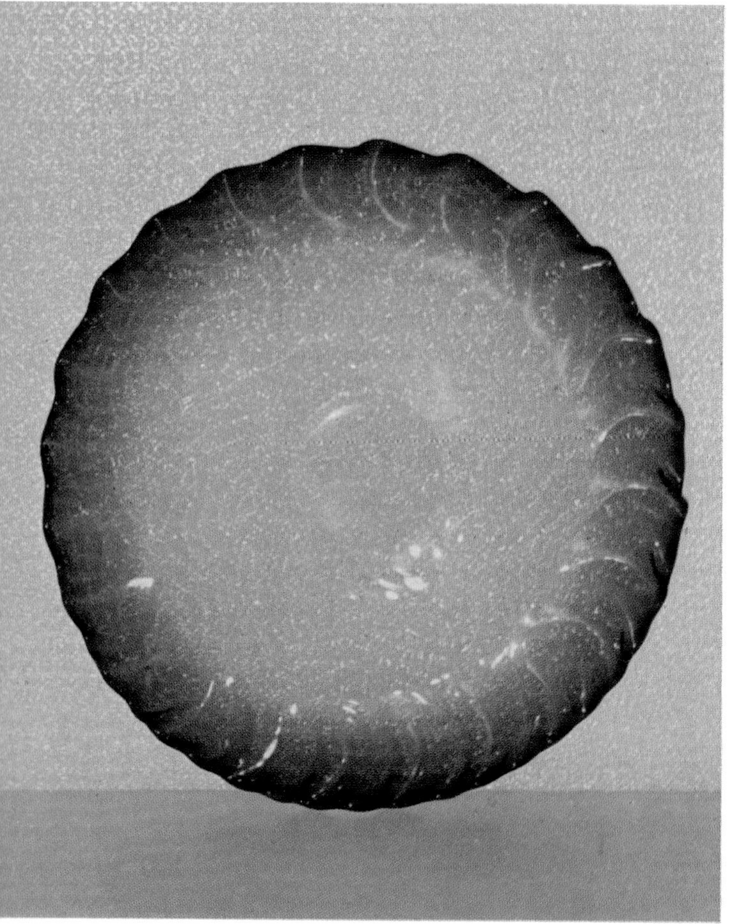

340. Alexandrite plate, 6″, collection of Mrs. Matt T. Donahue.

341. Alexandrite creamer and plate, 5 1/2", collection of Mr. and Mrs. C. W. Bray.

Text on p. 161

342. Silveria vase, Stevens and Williams Company, 11 1/2″, Milan Historical Museum.

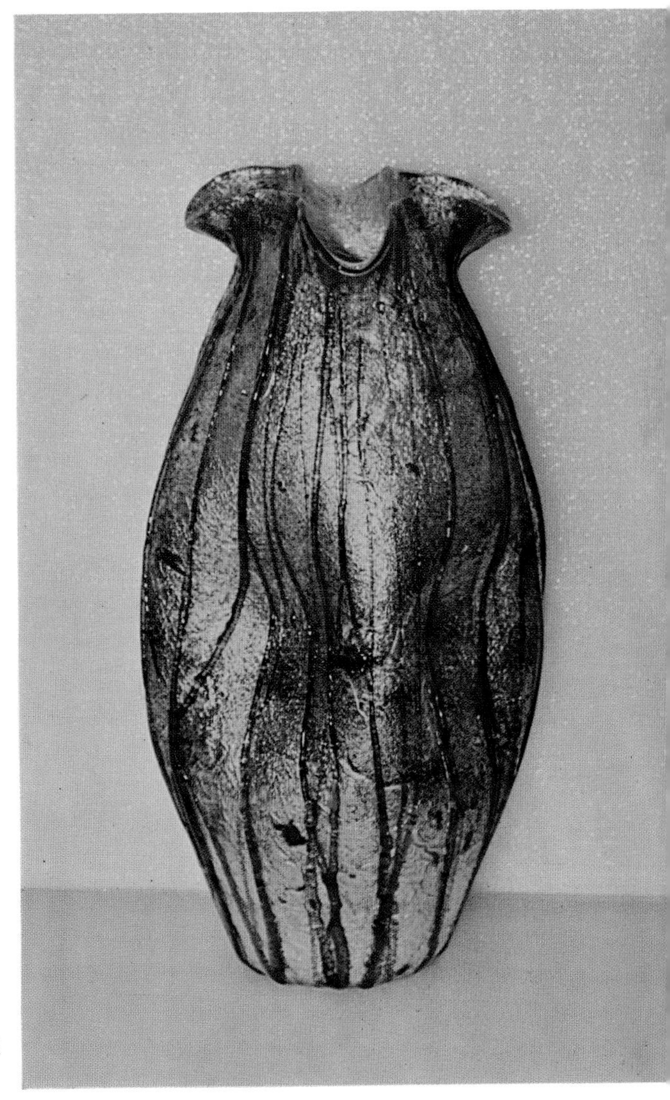

343. Silveria vase, Stevens and Williams Company, signed *S W*, 9″, collection of Mr. and Mrs. Gerry Philpot.

Text on p. 180

Northwood became director of the Stevens & Williams operation. For this reason the "attributed" cannot be too strongly stressed.

Miscellaneous English (continued)

Plate 344 showing a decorated satin finished amberina attributed to Thomas Webb & Sons is quite similar to Webb Peach Blow. There is, however, one very marked difference. In the Peach Blow ware, the outer casing shades from a cherry red to pink, while the amberina shades from the same cherry red to a yellow (Plate 88).

Gray Stan marked glass, Plate 351, was produced in the 1920's, and while many of the pieces were of limited shape, there was considerable use made of the cluthra type, inner decoration. Most of this work was experimental in nature and signed. At first glance it is very similar to Kimball's cluthra glass. The colors have a striking intensity.

The Moss Agate shown in Plate 349, attributed to Stevens and Williams, is similar in structure but less highly colored than the Moss Agate produced by Steuben. It should be noted, however, that Frederick Carder was the art director at Stevens & Williams prior to heading The Steuben Glass Company.

* * * * *

French

About 1875, with the emergence of Emile Galle, 1846–1904, as the leader, a new type of art in glass was evolved. The theme, "nature in glass," became the expression of the school of Galle, recognized master of this art form.

Whereas the English school is better known for its technical perfection in execution of design, the French school certainly makes us aware that shaded color masses, combined with flower portrayals in relief, were the distinctive features of art nouveau French glass. Insect, animal, and fish motifs were not uncommon in the work of this school. Featured in conjunction with cameo technique was the use of subtle enamel coloring on the cameos themselves as well as on the flat surface.

Plates pp. 190–91

For some fifteen years Galle specialized in producing pieces of individual importance until the more practical side of glass manufacturing made it imperative for him to modify his operation, enabling an increased quantity of work to reach the public. Individuality of every single work ceased, and while it is rare that we encounter duplicates, there was a pronounced similarity of style and decoration. The Galle operation continued until 1913, nine years after the death of its leader. In spite of the tremendous number of pieces finished at his factory, Emile Galle personally entered into the completion of the vast majority of the work. Impossible as this might seem, this is not an overstatement for it should always be remembered that Galle's life was devoted to a personal expression of the art found in nature.

Plates pp. 190ff.

A full coverage of the wide French field could encompass many books this size, as is also true in the Venetian, English, and general European areas. In an effort, however, to show a cross section of this particular group, we have endeavored to picture a diversified number of artist-workmen whose work you are likely to come across. A group from some eighteen different artists and factories was chosen, including the Belgium Val St. Lambert. Rene Lalique, whose individual works of art are classified in the field of jewelry originations, shortly after 1900 specialized in molded work and quantity production, primarily with a heavy acid or camphor-glass finish.

Plate p. 195

While this group seems to be numerically large, it is in reality only a representative minority of which we become increasingly aware as we delve into the French glass group. England, Bohemia, Italy, and the United States, on the other hand, are represented by their major factories, where we have a host of individual artist identifications.

* * * * *

Venetian

There is a history of some two thousand years of glassmaking in Italy. Venice has maintained an unparalleled continuity in the production of great glass, and remains to this day one of the major glass centers of the world.

Plates p. 198

A specialty of the Venetians is the Millefiore technique. Multi-colored glass rods were banded together and drawn out in narrow tubular shapes. Very thin cross-section slices were then made and imbedded in larger masses of glass which were subsequently brought to their ultimate shapes. Another approach to the use of the millefiore wafers was to lay them on a transparent glass and expand the piece, thus achieving vases with beautiful floral designs (Plate 382). In Plate 379 we notice inlay work consisting of numerous single color glass threads layed on and shaped to suggest a group of dragonflies in a cage. This particular piece was fashioned about 1895 and is signed by the artist.

It would not be an understatement to say that every type of glass construction and decoration, at one time or another, was used in Venice. Murano, a small island, only minutes by boat from Venice, has a small but unusually fine museum which houses examples of Venetian rarities. Filigree, or latticino glass, was another specialty of these workmen. The technical perfection and delicacy of their glass is a distinguishing feature of these wares.

* * * * *

Lithyalin

Plates p. 199

Lithyalin, a type of so-called stone glass, was produced in Bohemia about 1830, by Friedrich Egermann. Throughout the history of glass making, one of the cardinal aims has been to simulate the whole range of precious and semi-precious stones. Not only in color simulation was

Text cont. on p. 203

344. Amberina bowl, attributed to Thomas Webb and Sons, 4 1/2″, collection of Mr. and Mrs. Raymond Suppes.

345. Bronze glass vase, Thomas Webb and Sons, 5″, authors' collection.

346. Iridescent vase, Thomas Webb and Sons, 6 1/2″, collection of Mr. and Mrs. Gerry Philpot.

347. Intaglio-cut cased glass vase, attributed to Thomas Webb and Sons, 10 1/2″, authors' collection.

Text on p. 181

348. Silvered vase, signed *Hale Thomson, Patent, London,* 7″, collection of Mr. and Mrs. Raymond Suppes.

Text on pp. 180–81

349. Moss Agate vase, Stevens and Williams, 3 3/4″, authors' collection.

350. Richardson's vitrified glass pitcher, signed *Stourbridge 1850,* 9 3/4″, collection of Mr. and Mrs. Gerry Philpot.

351. Clutra chalice, signed *Gray Stan,* 10 1/2″, authors' collection.

Text on p. 184

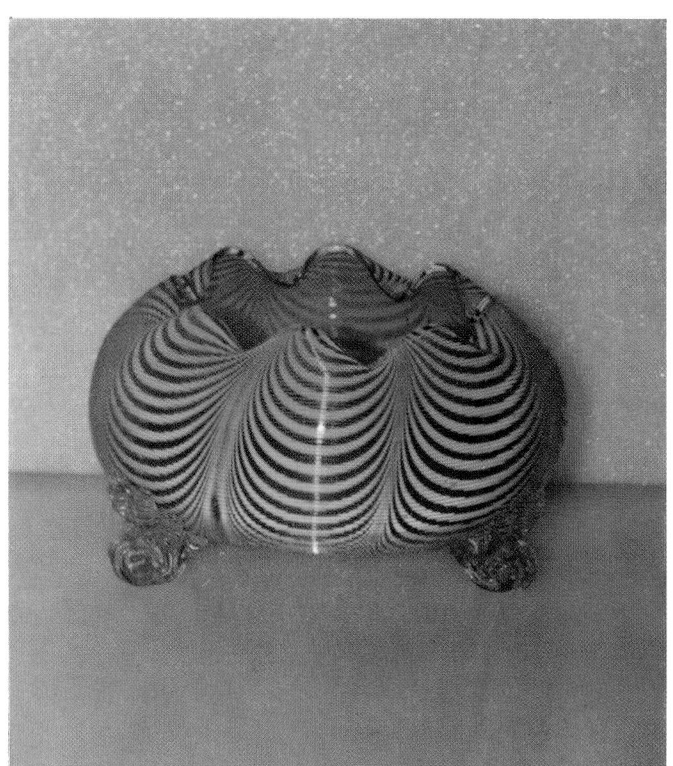

352. Threaded glass bowl with a berry prunt, 4″, collection of Mr. and Mrs. Gerry Philpot.

353. Ewer, pull-up pattern with a clear outer coating, attributed to Stevens and Williams Company, 12 1/4″, collection of Mr. and Mrs. Gerry Philpot.

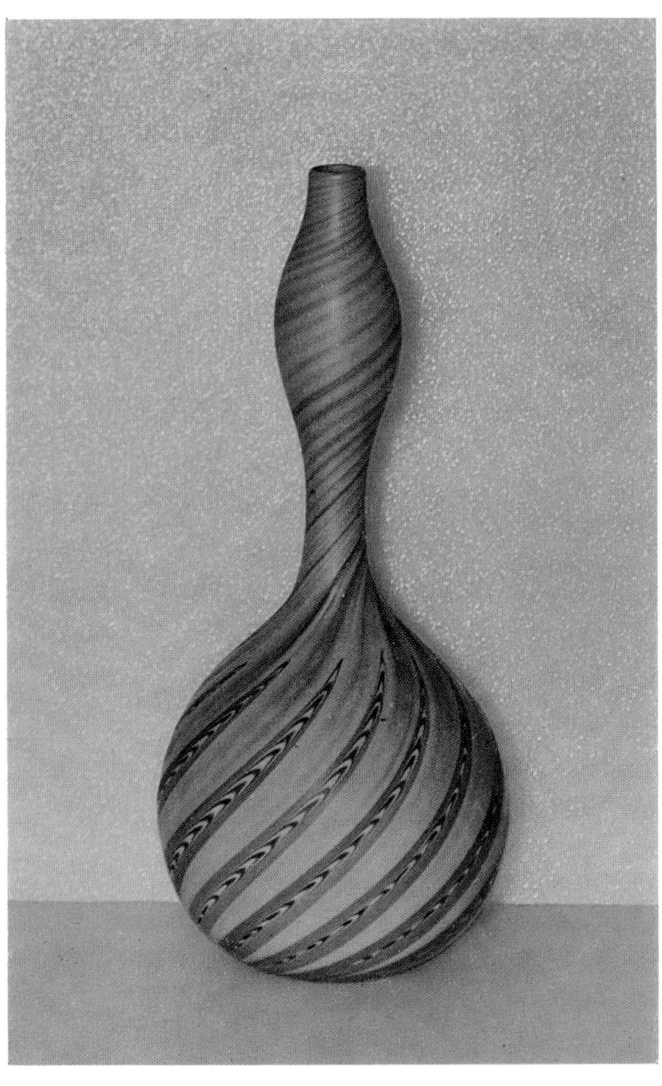

354. Gourd-shaped vase, satin finished, threaded pull-up, attributed to John Northwood, England, circa 1880, 10″, collection of Mr. and Mrs. Raymond Suppes.

Text on p. 181

355. French enamelled tumblers, signed *E. Galle, Nancy,* 4 1/2″, collection of Mr. and Mrs. Raymond Suppes.

356. French cameo Goblet, signed *Galle,* 8 1/4″, collection of Mr. and Mrs. J. Michael Pearson.

Text on p. 184

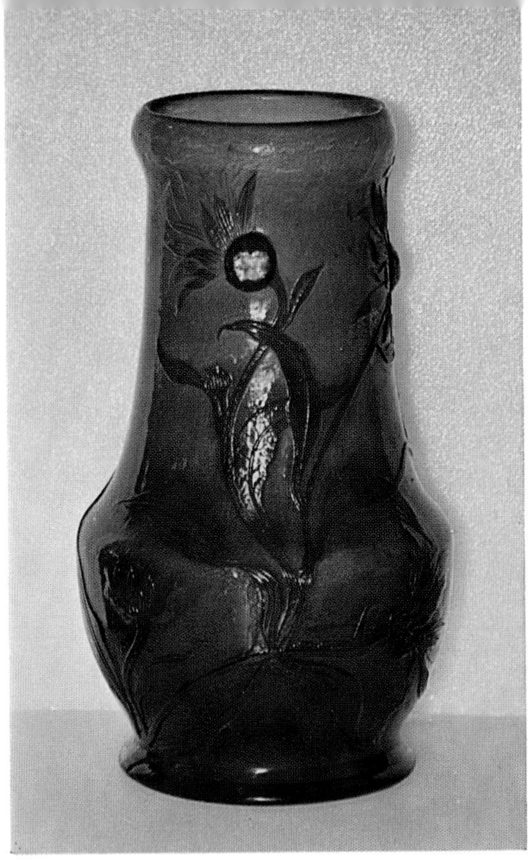

357. French cameo vase, signed *Crystallerie, E. Galle,* 11″, Chrysler Art Museum.

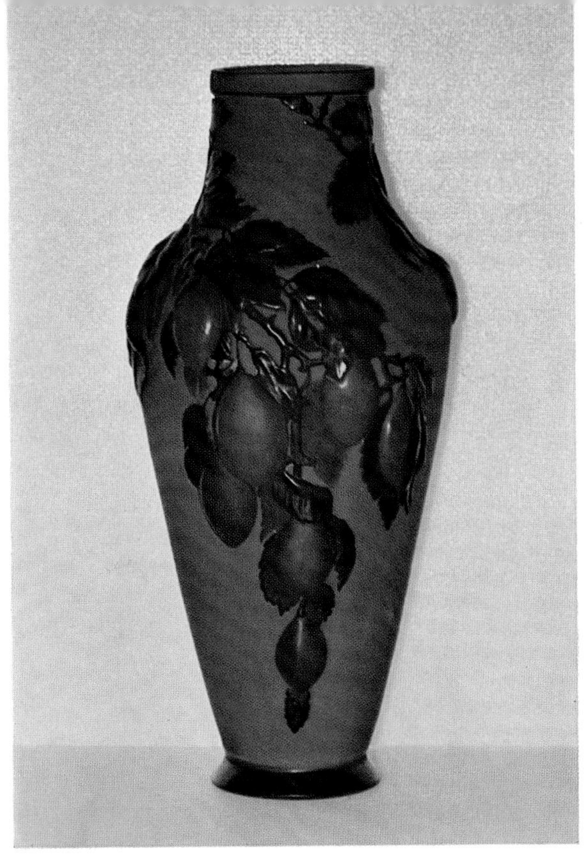

358. French cameo vase, signed *Galle,* 15 1/4″, Chrysler Art Museum.

359. French vase, signed *Galle,* 14″, collection of Mr. and Mrs. Raymond Suppes.

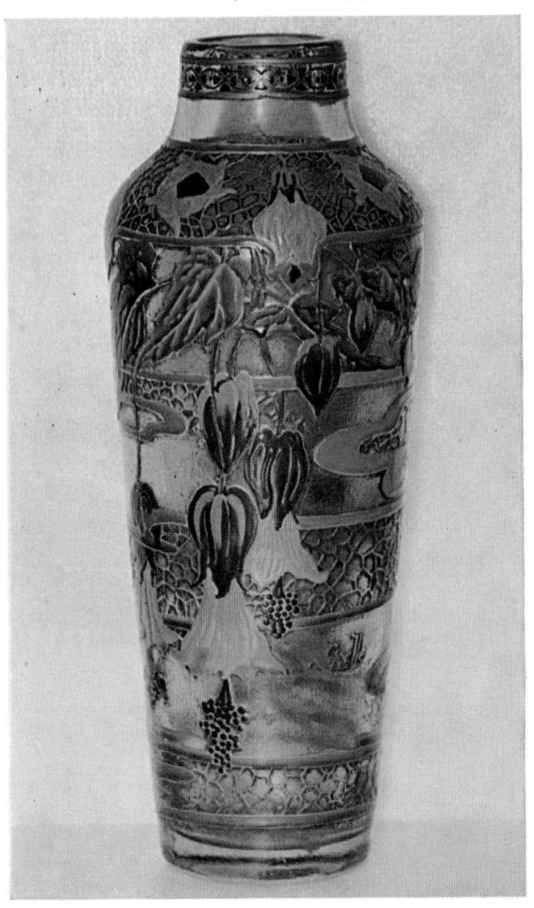

360. French cameo vase, signed *E. Galle, Nancy,* 14 1/4″, Chrysler Art Museum.

Text on p. 184

361. French Pate de Verre cameo technique ashtray, signed *A. Walter, Nancy*, 6″, Chrysler Art Museum.

362. French cameo basket, signed *Daum, Nancy*, 6 3/4″, Chrysler Art Museum.

363. French cameo vase, signed *DeVez*, 11″, Chrysler Art Museum.

364. French cameo vase, signed *Montjoye*, 11 1/2″, Chrysler Art Museum.

Text on p. 184

365. French Pate De Verre built-up cameo vase, signed *G. Argy-Rousseau*, 9″, collection of Mr. and Mrs. Raymond Suppes.

Text on p. 184

366. French cameo vase, signed *St. Louis,* 7″, collection of Mr. and Mrs. Raymond Suppes.

367. French cameo vase, signed *Muller Freres, Luneville.* 8 1/2″, collection of Mr. and Mrs. Raymond Suppes.

368. French cameo vase, signed *E. Rego,*11 3/4″, Chrysler Art Museum.

369. French cameo vase, signed *Richard,* 7 3/4″, collection of Mr. and Mrs. Raymond Suppes.

Text on p. 184

370. Val St. Lambert cameo glass vase decorated with enamelling, a product of Belgium's outstanding glass factory, signed *Val St. Lambert,* 16 1/2″, collection of Mr. and Mrs. Raymond Suppes.

Text on p. 184

371. French Pitcher, signed *Schneider,* 6 1/2″, collection of Mr. and Mrs. Raymond Suppes.

372. French Glass vase, not to be confused with porcelain, signed *Sevres,* 5 1/4″, collection of Mr. and Mrs. Raymond Suppes.

373. French cameo vase, signed *D'Argental,* 11 3/4″, Chrysler Art Museum.

374. French cameo vase, signed *De L'Arte Nancy,* 10″, collection of Mr. and Mrs. Raymond Suppes.

Text on p. 184

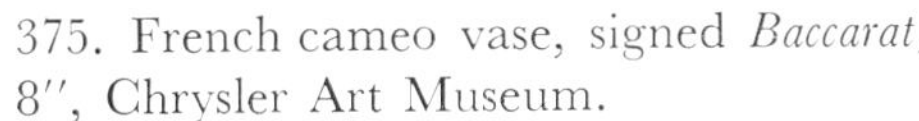

375. French cameo vase, signed *Baccarat,* 8″, Chrysler Art Museum.

376. French cameo and enamel decorated vase, signed *LeGras,* 6 1/2″, Chrysler Art Museum.

377. French cameo ewer, signed *Roux Chalon A. R. Saone,* 9″, Chrysler Art Museum.

378. French cameo vase, signed *DeLatte,* 8 1/4″, Chrysler Art Museum.

Text on p. 184

379. Venetian vase with millefiore application, circa 1895, signed *E. Zarovien, Murano,* 8″, authors' collection.

380. Venetian cream pitcher with millefiore decoration, 4″, collection of Mr. and Mrs. Raymond Suppes.

381. Venetial vase with millefiore inlay, 7 3/4″, collection of Mr. and Mrs. Raymond Suppes.

382. Venetian vase with millefiore and other inlaid decoration rolled into outer surface, circa 1895, 8″, authors' collection.

Text on p. 185

383. Bohemian Lithyalin bowl, produced by Friedrich Egerman, circa 1835, 3″, collection of Mr. and Mrs. Raymond Suppes.

384. Bohemian Lithyalin vase, produced by Friedrich Egerman, circa 1835, 15″, authors' collection.

385. Bhoemian Lithyalin vase, produced by Friedrich Egerman, circa 1835, 9″, collection of Sally A. Rose.

Text on p. 185

386. Peloton "shredded cocoanut" or "spaghetti" covered bowl produced by Wilhelm Kralik Bohemia, circa 1880, 7″, collection of Mr. and Mrs. Gerry Philpot.

387. Peloton "shredded cocoanut" or "spaghetti" plate, manufactured by Wilhelm Kralik, Bohemia, circa 1880, 7 1/4″, collection of Mr. and Mrs. Raymond Suppes.

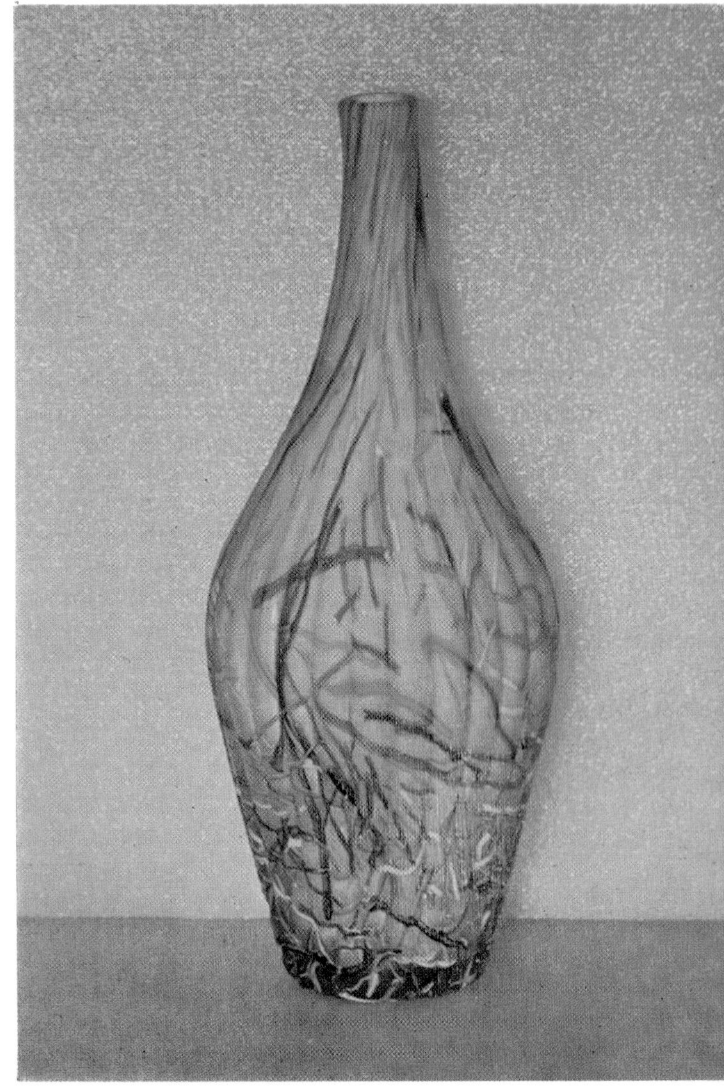

388. Peloton "shredded cocoanut" or "spaghetti" vase, 9 1/4″, Milan Historical Museum.

Text on p. 203

389. Bohemian Moser bowl, single color, signed *Moser-Alexandrite,* 4 3/4″, collection of Mr. and Mrs. Gerry Philpot.

390. Bohemian Moser vase with enamelled decoration, signed *Moser,* 10 1/4″, collection of Mr. and Mrs. Gerry Philpot.

Text on p. 203

391. Bohemian vase with cameo decoration on double layered glass, with white enamelling fired on, 5 1/2″, collection of Mr. and Mrs. Raymond Suppes.

Text on p. 203

considerable effort expended, but also in the desire to create in glass the striations and graining that enhances the beauty of polished agates. Egermann succeeded not only in offering a finished piece of glass suggestive of polished stone but in addition turned this ware out in many eye pleasing shapes.

Lithyalin (continued)

Of course the finish is glossy, for otherwise the multi-colored lines would be lost in an acid treatment. As might be noticed in Plate 383, very interesting greenish-gray linings are typical of his product. Reds, browns, grayish-cast greens predominate, being set off by black. Broad and flat polishing tools were used, resulting in flat surfaces an inch or so in width, totally surrounding the finished piece. Actual width of the surface cutting was normally dependent on the circumference of the work. We have had four-sided bottles in this ware, and it is of course conceivable there could be a minimum of three sides, however, it is usual to find a minimum of eight flat surfaces on the majority of Egermann's Lithyalin.

* * * * *

Peloton

Plates p. 200

A variety of shapes, mostly utilitarian in form, appear in Peloton glass. Of European origin, the ware normally has a transparent colored or clear body. Small threads of glass of the same color or a hodgepodge of numerous contrasting colors were rolled into the surface of the piece. Opaque white glass with striking colored wire-like glass thread layed on in a hit-or-miss pattern are extremely desirable. Rather heavy enameled surface decoration also seems to have been added in an effort to create a busier and novel effect.

* * * * *

Moser

Plates p. 201

One of the finer European glassmen of the early 1900's was Kolo Moser, a designer as well as decorator. Fine Moser pieces may be recognized by their exquisite and detailed enameling (Plate 390). Another innovation in amethyst transparent glass is seen in Plate 389. This particular work usually carries the mark "Alexandrite" underfoot, along with Moser. A one-color ware, this should not be confused with the three-shaded work attributed to Webb, as well as Stevens & Williams, in the same period. The only similarity is in the name.

* * * * *

Simulated Cameo

Plate p. 202

As seen in Plate 391, simulated cameo decoration is usually achieved by extremely fine white enamel work on overlay vases. The high cost of producing English cameo encouraged Bohemian sources to search for a cheaper method of producing work with the same surface decorative effect. There is nothing crude in the execution, but unfortunately this competed with and depressed the fine English cameo market.

Text cont. on p. 206

392. Austrian vase, signed *Loetz Austria,* 6 1/4″, Chrysler Art Museum.

393. Austrian vase, signed *Loetz Austria,* 4 1/2″, Chrysler Art Museum.

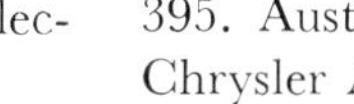

394. Austrian vase, signed *Loetz,* 5 1/4″, collection of Mr. and Mrs. Gerry Philpot.

395. Austrian vase, signed *Loetz Austria,* 6″, Chrysler Art Museum.

Text on p. 206

396. Austrian flower form, signed *Loetz Austria,* 12 1/2″, Chrysler Art Museum.

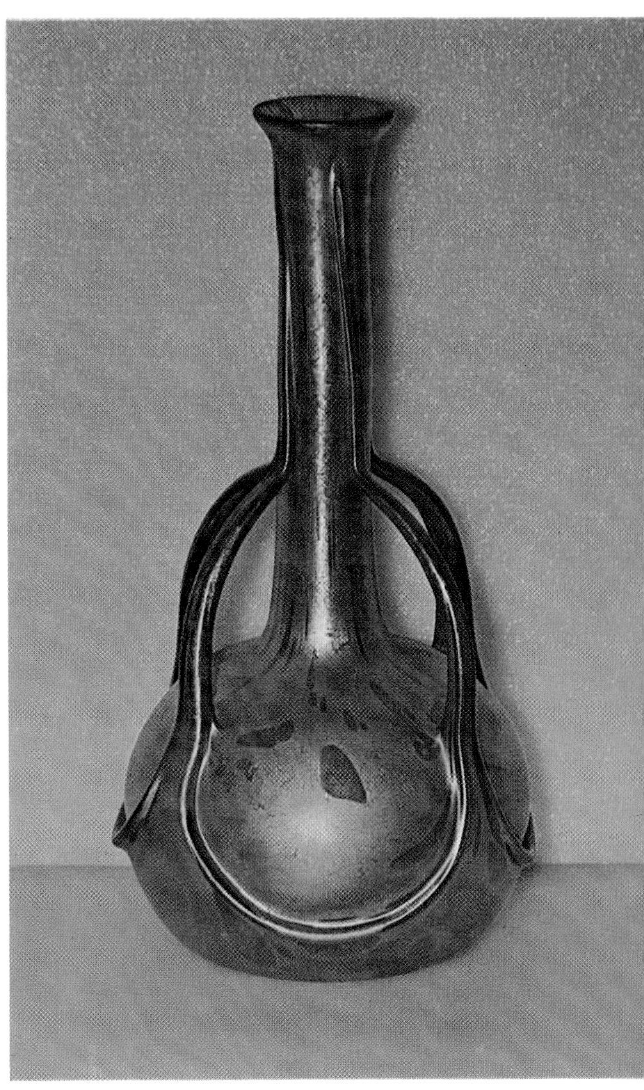

397. Austrian vase, signed *Loetz,* 12″, collection of Mr. and Mrs. Gerry Philpot.

Text on p. 206

Loetz

Loetz glass, manufactured in Austria, is also known by the name of Loetz Witwe. Very little of this glass is marked, but when it is signed it will usually be identified as "Loetz," "Loetz-Austria," or "Austria," with a pair of crossed arrows in a circle.

Plates p. 204–5

Great similarity in shape and surface iridescence is noted between Loetz and many of the finest wares produced in the American art glass field. All the pieces illustrated bear an identifying signature. Certainly the rare flower form (Plate 396) might very well compare with the best of Tiffany in this particular shape. Possibly the most important clue to the identification of unsigned Loetz is the type of decoration that seems to stand out "on the the surface." Similar Tiffany decorative effect would suggest the decoration as coming from within the glass itself. See Plate 392.

Plate 393, with the lily pad type of overlay is quite typical of Loetz. Iridescence as applied by Loetz is of extremely good quality with nothing left unfinished, quality wise. A combination iridescent and glossy finishing, appearing on the same piece, as seen in Plate 394, is usually restricted to Loetz. This same type of finish is alien to Tiffany.

Signed pieces of Loetz should be examined carefully on the underfoot, ground pontil area. Here a particularly clear color inherent to the basic color of the piece may be seen. Many other pieces attributed to Loetz do not have a ground pontil and were finished by pressing into a mold.

New collectors will undoubtedly find it difficult to differentiate between unsigned Loetz and many of the fine American wares, but it should take only a short time for most collector-students of glass to determine the origin correctly.

* * * * *

Aventurine, Spangle, and Spatter glass are three different types of glass.

Aventurine, Spangle, and Spatter

Aventurine is a fine sparkling material suggestive of sprinkled gold dust. It was produced by various mixes of copper in yellow glass. The finished pieces of Aventurine glass were then broken and crushed into various sizes, for use as a decorative material. Other colors in Aventurine may be found.

Plate p. 209

Plates p. 208

Spangle particles normally consist of small pieces of mica coated with gold, silver, nickel, or copper. This plated mica was then broken down into sizes suitable for use.

Plates p. 209

Spatter particles consist only of small pieces of different colored glass.

It is usual for any one of these three varied types of fragments to be entrapped between two layers of glass, although they could in fact be merely applied to the outer surface of a one-layered piece of glass and then rolled into the surface. This, however, is quite infrequent. While the inner layer of glass upon which these materials are layed is almost always opaque, primarily as a background to show up the sparkling colors, the outer layer of glass is very often of a transparent color, in addition to being clear. This colored outer layer may change the overall shading of the complete piece as shown in Plate 403 with its blue casing, signed "W. & C." Plate p. 209

Vasa Murrhina glass is a mixture of two or three of the above items, although this name is also mistakenly applied individually to Aventurine, Spatter, or Spangle glass.

Aventurine, in large pieces, was sold commercially to any glass house wishing to purchase it. Coated mica flakes, or spangle, was also easy to obtain. Because of these facts, and since Spatter glass was a frequent surplus item found in every glass manufactory, it is not surprising to realize that almost every maker of any size at all, any place in the world, undoubtedly turned out some quantity of this attractive ware.

In Plate 399, a beautiful effect of spangle layed upon a rainbow background shows just what can be achieved by a little ingenuity. The blown-mold pattern pitcher, Plate 402, also illustrates another combination of design.

* * * * *

Libbey

Plates p. 211

The Libbey Glass Company became the successor to the New England Glass Company, Cambridge, Massachusetts, when New England closed down in 1888 and the new operation opened in Toledo, Ohio. It still operates there today, very well known, and catering to the large industrial field.

In addition to their amberina, mentioned under that grouping, Libbey was not above turning out many experimental pieces, handblown, as well as molded. Plate 404 is just such a piece. If you will note the signature, it reads "cut glass." This is not a typographical error nor a factory mistake, inasmuch as we have seen other pieces so marked. The other two objects, a candlestick (Plate 406) and tazza (Plate 405) are hand blown shapes of colored glass threading layed on and rolled smooth into the surface. These two are both glossy finish, while the small bowl is acid finish. Any signed piece of Libbey that appears should be acquired by the collector, for although they are rather uninspired in form, colorwise they are quite true, and certainly extremely rare.

* * * * *

Star Holly

Plates p. 212

Star Holly glass, manufactured by the Imperial Glass Company, Bellaire, Ohio, had a very limited production during the early part of the 20th century. In the milk glass field, this ware was mold manufactured, and other than the colored sections, is of a glossy finish.

Text cont. on p. 210

398. Spangled mica flake creamer, 5″, Milan Historical Museum.

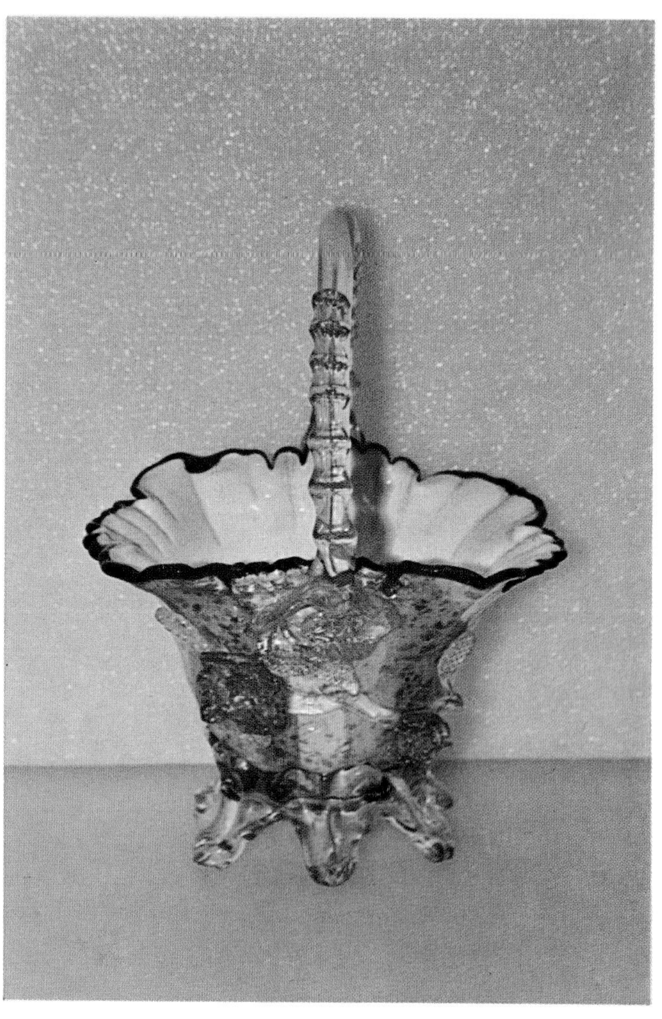

399. Spangled rainbow basket, overlay decorated, 8″, collection of Mr. and Mrs. Gerry Philpot.

Text on p. 206

400. Spatter covered jar, 6 1/4″, collection of Mr. and Mrs. Raymond Suppes.

401. Spatter diamond pattern mug, 4 1/2″, collection of Mr. and Mrs. Raymond Suppes.

402. Aventurine pitcher, 7″, collection of Mr. and Mrs. Gerry Philpot.

403. Spatter vase, signed *W & C*, 10 1/2″, authors' collection.

Text on pp. 206–7

Three colors, blue, green, and coral, varying in depth according to the density of the pigments, were used in an effort to simulate English Wedgwood. When the pieces were partially completed the various colors were brushed on and had very little surface absorption. Due to the considerable amount of handwork needed for the actual coloring of the pieces, together with the seemingly difficult means of controlling the shade, only a limited number of these pieces ever reached the market. Here again, as in most molded ware of this period, shapes show more of a useful nature rather than striving for "art" forms.

* * * * *

Findlay Onyx

Plates p. 213

Findlay Onyx glass, manufactured by the Dalzell, Gilmore, Leighton Company, Findlay, Ohio, about 1889, is commonly spoken of as "Findlay Glass." A molded rather than hand blown process was used to establish the raised pattern as well as the ultimate shape and size.

But small variance exists from one piece to another in the same shape. On the contrary, however, it is difficult to pick up any two similar shaped pieces, and find them to be of the same shade. In addition to the syrup (Plate 410), which is the color most common in the various shapes, we have endeavored to picture some other rather interesting color combinations. Lustre colors applied to the patterns are usually in contrast to the main body of the piece, and the numerous shadings were controlled by the heat of firing. We have at one time or another come across a very wide range of colors and color combinations.

Almost all of the ware was produced in utilitarian shapes, and, while susceptible to many small chips around the open rims, are in remarkably fine condition when we realize they were made for daily useage. It should not be overlooked that practically any color, other than that shown in the syrup, is exceedingly scarce, including the almost white pitcher (Plate 412).

* * * * *

Pink Slag

Plates p. 214

Pink Slag glass in the inverted fan and feather pattern is attributed to the Indiana Tumbler and Goblet Company, Greentown, Indiana. Only a small quantity was produced, and richly colored pieces of pink, shading to white, are quite rare. Molded shapes for utilitarian purposes were offered in the glossy finish just as they emerged from the fire. Cruets with the original stopper (Plate 413) are among the most sought after rarities in the Pink Slag group, although any of this ware in a good, deep, pink color is highly desirable.

* * * * *

Holly Amber

Plates p. 215
Text cont. on p. 219

Holly Amber glass, produced by the Indiana Tumbler and Goblet Co., Greentown, Indiana, enjoyed remarkable acceptance by the public. This molded ware was offered in a glossy finish with various opalescent to golden brown shadings. A remarkably warm glow is one of

404. Satin bowl, Libbey Glass Company, signed *Libbey Cut Glass, Toledo,* 2 1/2″, collection of Mr. and Mrs. Gerry Philpot.

405. Tazza, Libbey Glass Company, signed *Libbey,* 6″, collection of J. Michael Pearson.

406. Candlestick with pink feather design, Libbey Glass Company, signed *Libbey,* 6″, collection of J. Michael Pearson.

Text on p. 207

407. Star Holly bowl, Imperial Glass Company, signed *I. G.*, 8 3/4″, authors' collection.

408. Star Holly handled sugar bowl and saucer, Imperial Glass Company, signed *I. G.*, 3 1/2″, authors' collection.

409. Star Holly goblet, Imperial Glass Company, signed *I. G.*, 6″, collection of Mrs. Robert Baker, Sr.

Text on p. 207

410. Findlay onyx syrup, 7″, collection of Mrs. Robert Baker, Sr.

411. Findlay onyx raspberry colored spooner, 4″, collection of Dr. and Mrs. Walter Donahue.

412. Findlay onyx pitcher, 8″, collection of Mrs. Robert Baker, Sr.

Text on p. 210

413. Pink Slag cruet, 6 1/2″, collection of Mr. and Mrs. C. W. Bray.

414. Pink Slag pitcher, 8 1/4″, collection of Mr. and Mrs. C. W. Bray.

415. Pink Slag covered sugar and creamer, 5 1/2″, collection of Mr. and Mrs. C. W. Bray.

Text on p. 210

416. Holly Amber covered compote, 9″, collection of Mr. and Mrs. C. W. Bray.

417. Holly Amber syrup, 6″, collection of Mr. and Mrs. C. W. Bray.

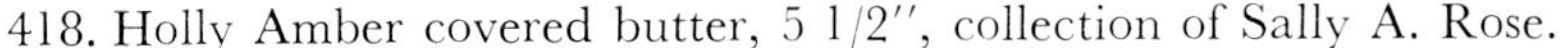

418. Holly Amber covered butter, 5 1/2″, collection of Sally A. Rose.

Text on p. 210

419. Fry vase with amethyst handle, H. C. Fry Glass Company, 8″, collection of Mrs. Robert Baker, Sr.

420. Fry candlesticks, opal glass having blue wafers and sage green diagonal threading, H. C. Fray Glass Company, 12″, collection of Mr. and Mrs. Raymond Suppes.

421. Fry covered coffee pot with blue handle and finial, H. C. Fry Glass Company, 9 1/2″, collection of Mr. and Mrs. Raymond Suppes.

Text on p. 219

422. Joseph Locke celery vase, ivory glass with maize pattern, designed by Joseph Locke, W. L. Libbey & Son, 6 3/4″, collection of Mrs. Robert Baker, Sr.

Text on pp. 219–20

423. Joseph Locke pitcher with a typical grape motif etching, signed *Locke Art,* 13 1/2″, authors' collection.

Text on p. 220

the most noticeable traits of Holly Amber. Shapewise, the pieces were of utilitarian form. Flatware with a grayish white, pearlescent center is more sought after than those pieces in which there is a predominance of brown. The beautiful shading pictured in the covered butter (Plate 418) is a fine example of the coloration most desired. It should not be overlooked that a small quantity of "clear" Holly, was produced. Without any color, as the name implies, the molds were the same ones as those used for Holly Amber.

Holly Amber (continued)

* * * * *

Fry

Plates p. 216

Fry glass, in the art glass field, represented a very limited operation for the H.C. Fry Glass Company, Rochester, Pennsylvania. One of the better glass houses in the production of cut glass during the first quarter of the 20th century, they were always noted for the brilliance of the glass itself as well as for their fine cutting ability. This would undoubtedly account for the beautiful opalescence of their art pieces in color.

Opal ware by Fry could very easily be confused with similar glass manufactured by the Steuben Glass Works. Certainly the contrasting colors used in conjunction with the opal are practically the same as the Steuben jades. One factor alone would never permit anyone ever to mistake the origin of the two wares: Steuben invariably made the main body of their pieces in the solid jade colors and used the opal glass for handles and other trim, while Fry glass is just the opposite. The main body of all their ware was opal glass, and the trim was in color. As a matter of interest, the pair of candlesticks (Plate 420) has trim consisting of a pale green diagonal threading, and the wafers are a royal blue. Many of the Fry pieces are likely to be found in interesting variations of the shapes normally offered for commercial use, as you will note in Plate 421. In addition, seemingly many of their shapes are slightly more bulbous than usual, albeit most attractive. It would not be practical to refuse pieces unmarked, as this was quite the rule, rather than the exception.

* * * * *

Maize

Plate p. 217

Maize glass, sold by the W.L. Libbey & Son, Company, Toledo, Ohio, was another one of the vast array of glass patented by Joseph Locke, formerly with the predecessor New England Glass Company. This ware, offered to the public in 1889, is a pressed glass with a glossy finish except where Maize leaves fan out from the foot. These leaves normally are of a painted green, although they are seen in red and blue. Plate 422 shows an opaque white body, but it should be remembered that it is also found in light green or yellow, transparent except for the leaf work. Different color stains were applied to the transparent glass but evidently had small penetration power as most pieces are somewhat worn in this respect. Gold decoration fired at a low temperature, also quite perishable, was used. This ware, produced for a large public consumption, was made in shapes for household use.

Undoubtedly one of the outstanding artist workmen of the past hundred years, Joseph Locke, aged ninety when he died in 1936, had been recognized for his achievements in all phases of the glass industry. Patents in his name were taken out for Amberina, Plated Amberina, Green Opaque, Pomona, and Agata, to mention only a few. These were in turn taken over by his employer, the New England Glass Company, with whom he became associated when he left England to come to the United States about 1880.

Joseph Locke

Plates pp. 217–18

For a short period he travelled west to be employed by The Libbey Glass Company, Toledo, Ohio, successors to the New England Glass Company. This relationship was of short duration. He next moved to Pittsburgh, Pennsylvania, where he lived with his family for some thirty-five years. Joseph Locke, famous for his color creations, was also recognized in England as well as in the United States as one of the finest engravers. Thus it is not surprising to find that upon settling down in Pittsburgh, Locke devoted much of his time to designing and etching. Locke did not blow his own glass, but rather purchased blanks, and from time to time did fanciful picture work in a free-hand etching style. An "Uncle Remus" series, with various cartoons of Peter Rabbit and Br'er Fox is highly amusing. We show in Plate 423 a pitcher with the allover "grape and vine" pattern for which Locke was quite well known. Floral patterns also appealed to this master engraver. Occasionally his pieces were signed "Joe Locke," but the usual identifying mark is "Locke Art." The pieces are not signed underfoot but are signed in random positions, the signature being worked into the overall pattern itself. Etching of his mark is in very small letters and can very easily present a challenge of an hour's searching for his mark, even on small pieces. This work was done, with few exceptions, on clear glass and in only a very limited quantity. The piece in Plate 423 is quite typical in shape of the pitchers upon which Joseph Locke did most of his more impressive etching.

MUSEUMS

Alfred University Museum, Alfred, New York
The Bennington Museum, Bennington, Vermont
The Brooklyn Museum of Art, Brooklyn, New York
The Chrysler Museum of Art, Provincetown, Massachusetts
Cooper Union Museum, New York City, New York
The Corning Museum of Glass, Corning, New York
The Ford Museum, Dearborn, Michigan.
The Metropolitan Museum of Art, New York, New York
The Milan Historical Museum, Milan, Ohio
The Morgan's Museum of Art Glass, Groveland, California, Highway 120 at the northern entrance to Yosemite National Park
The Morse Gallery of Art, Rollins College, Winter Park, Florida
The Museum of Contemporary Crafts—Museum of Modern Art, New York City, New York
Rockwell Galleries, Corning, New York
Sandwich Historical Society Museum, Sandwich, Massachusetts
The Smithsonian Institution, Washington, D.C.
The Toledo Museum of Art, Toledo, Ohio

OWNERSHIP LIST

Following is a list of the individuals and the museums whose pieces of art glass are illustrated in this book. The numbers following the names refer to plates and not to pages.

Armentrout, Frances D., 211, 229, 244–45, 247, 248, 251, 253–54, 256
Baker, Mrs. Robert, Sr., 409–10, 412, 419, 422
Berger, Mr. and Mrs. Bernard, 153
Bray, Mr. and Mrs. C. W., 1, 14, 31–32, 37, 43, 46, 78–87, 90, 98, 135, 341, 413–17
Chrysler Art Museum, Front., 3–4, 8, 53, 61, 70–71, 89, 101, 107, 113, 124–25, 127, 130, 144, 160, 182, 194, 198, 203, 216–19, 221–24, 226, 233, 242, 246, 250, 252, 357–58, 360–64, 368, 373, 275–78, 392–93, 395–96
Collin, Mr. and Mrs. Milton, 154
Corning Museum of Glass, 73, 180, 273, 290–91
Donahue, James N., 13
Donahue, Mrs. Matt T., 16, 47, 72, 96, 118, 170, 188, 284, 287, 289, 340
Donahue, Dr. and Mrs. Walter, 39, 64, 99, 155, 172, 186, 240, 336, 411
Dubrow, Mr. and Mrs. Jerome, 423.
Eisenberg, Helen, 137, 139, 145, 149, 157, 162–63, 167, 171, 175–76, 184, 196, 199, 200, 202, 205, 208–10, 214
Favorito, Mr. and Mrs. Joseph, 156
Feld, Maud B., 5, 29, 48–50, 56, 58, 69, 76, 91–92, 97, 100, 121, 150, 169, 181, 238–39, 241, 314, 321, 330, 334
Gabler, Arthur, 313, 316
Gerstein, Mr. and Mrs. Barry, 220, 225
Gore, Mr. and Mrs. E. F., 40–42, 44, 65, 77
Grover, Mr. and Mrs. Ray, 105, 108, 133, 257, 317–18, 325, 328, 333, 345, 347, 349, 351, 379, 382, 384, 403, 407–8, 423
Hegarty, Mr. and Mrs. L. C., 24

BIBLIOGRAPHY

BARRET, RICHARD CARTER. *Identification of American Art Glass.*

BEARD, GEOFFREY W. *Nineteenth Century Cameo Glass.*

DANIEL, DOROTHY. *Cut and Engraved Glass,* 1771–1905.

DARR, PATRICK T. *A Guide to Art and Pattern Glass.*

ERICSON, ERIC E. *A Guide to Colored Steuben Glass,* 1903–1933.

FELD, STUART P. "Nature in Her Most Seductive Aspects," *Metropolitan Museum of Art Bulletin* (November, 1962).

HERRICK, RUTH. *Greentown Glass.*

HOTCHKISS, JOHN F. *Carder's Steuben Glass.*

Journal of Glass Studies (The Corning Museum of Glass), volumes 2 and 5.

KLINETOB, DARWIN. *Steuben Glass Catalogue* (republished),

KOCH, ROBERT. *Louis C. Tiffany, Rebel in Glass.*

LAGERBERG, TED AND VI. *Collectible Glass.*

LEE, RUTH WEBB. *Nineteenth Century Art Glass.*

LEE, RUTH WEBB. *Victorian Glass.*

LINDSEY, BESSIE M. *American Historical Glass.*

Louis Comfort Tiffany, 1848–1933. New York: Museum of Contemporary Crafts of the American Craftsmen's Council.

MARIACHER, G. *Italian Blown Glass.*

McKEARIN, HELEN AND GEORGE S. *Two Hundred Years of American Blown Glass.*

New Bedford Board of Trade Report (1889).

New England Glass Company. Toledo Museum of Art.

PHILPOT, CECILY AND GERRY. *Creations by Carder of Steuben.*

POLAK, ADA. *Modern Glass.*

REVI, ALBERT CHRISTIAN. *American Pressed Glass and Figure Bottles.*

REVI, ALBERT CHRISTIAN. *Nineteenth Century Glass.*

RHEIMS, MAURICE. *L;Objet,* 1900.

SCHRYVER, ELKA. *Glass and Crystal,* volumes 1 and 2.

Shull, Thelma. *Victorian Antiques.*
Speenburgh, Gertrude. *The Arts of the Tiffanys.*
Tiffany, Louis C. *The Art Work of Louis C. Tiffany.*
Vavra, J. R. *Five Thousand Years of Glassmaking.*
Wakefield, Hugh. *Nineteenth Century British Glass.*
Watkins, Lura Woodside. *Cambridge Glass.*
Works of Art by Louis Comfort Tiffany. The Morse Gallery of Art.

INDEX

All numerals refer to pages. Those in Roman type are for the text, while those in italics are for the plates.